FRIEND WHO...

By America's
Teens and
the Experts
at KidsPeace

Edited by
Anna Radev

Hazelden Publishing   Center City, Minnesota

Hazelden
Center City, Minnesota 55012-0176
1-800-328-0094
1-651-213-4590 (fax)
www.hazelden.org

Cover and interior design by David Farr, ImageSmythe
Print production by ImageSmythe, St. Paul, Minnesota
Cover and interior photos by Mike Krivit, Krivit Photography

Editor's note The stories and characters found in this book were created by the authors to represent common problems and experiences of preteens and teenagers. Any resemblance to specific persons, living and dead, or specific events is coincidental. This book is sold with the understanding that the publisher and author are not rendering individual psychological services to the reader. If such services are necessary, please consult an appropriate professional.

Library of Congress Cataloging-in-Publication Data
I've got this friend who— : advice for teens and their friends on
alcohol, drugs, eating disorders, risky behavior, and more / by America's teens and
the experts at KidsPeace ; edited by Anna Radev.
    p. cm.
 Includes bibliographical references and index.
 ISBN 978-1-59285-458-5 (softcover)
 1. Teenagers—Psychology. 2. Teenagers—Substance use. 3.
Teenagers—Alcohol use. 4. Eating disorders in adolescence. I. Radev,
Anna. II. KidsPeace.
 HQ796.I85 2007
 613.8—dc22
                              2007032822

11   10   09   08   07   1   2   3   4   5   6

CONTENTS

**FOREWORD**

by Chris Beckman, former cast member of MTV's *The Real World: Chicago* and author of *Clean*

GROWING UP TODAY IS NO EASY TASK. Believe me, I know! Especially since the challenges of my early teens led me down a path that took more than a decade to overcome. I remember thinking my whole life had crumbled. Drinking, drugs, and other things I couldn't control all but wiped out my teens. I was finally able to pull myself together and undo some of the damage, but it took time. I got clean at twenty-three and felt like I was still thirteen emotionally. I wrote the book *Clean: A New Generation in Recovery Speaks Out* to give teens a firsthand look at what it means to face the challenges I faced and what it takes to overcome them. I hoped sharing my experiences would help other teens avoid some of my mistakes and get a better head start on becoming adults.

Childhood is a magical time. Being a kid is great because you see the best in the world, you expect only good things to happen, and you trust others without question. You see the beauty and magic in everything— you're oblivious to all the dangers and bad things the world is capable of throwing at you. That starts to change as you get older and realize the world isn't always good and kind. Sadly, you lose a little of that wide-eyed innocence and wonderment that make childhood so great. But what you gain is knowledge, wisdom, and greater control over your destiny— sometimes without even realizing it.

The teen years can be an exciting and exhilarating time of self-discovery. But they're also a terrifying time of walking down a winding road you've never walked before, not knowing where it will take you or what dangers might be just around the corner. There's a whole new set of struggles and challenges at that age, from the smallest ones, like what clothes to wear, to life-and-death situations.

While none of us can hope to make all the right choices, we can pay attention to road signs that help point us in the right direction. That's what this book, *I've Got This Friend Who...*, is all about. It offers good advice from America's teens themselves and some of the country's top experts, who work every day on the frontlines with kids who've crashed on the road of life and have the bumps and bruises to prove it. The book offers proven advice—tips and tools to help you through a problem or tough issue—lots of encouragement, and important information about where to find the best resources. Best of all, the book's written in a way we all get—just as if we were talking to our friends. And that's what we need when we're having a hard time, right?

Nobody's perfect and we all make mistakes. Some mistakes help us learn, grow, become wiser, and build character and strength. But others have no benefit at all and destroy all the good things we might have in our lives. Those mistakes—like some of the ones I made growing up—aren't worth making, and if you can avoid them, you'll be a lot healthier and happier.

I've Got This Friend Who... is a good handbook for older kids and teens that can help you expect, avoid, or get over the biggest bumps on the road of life and the costly mistakes they can cause. This book gets my thumbs-up. Good luck and happy travels!

PREFACE

THIS BOOK TOOK 125 YEARS and 500,000 contributors to write. It sounds like a fantastic claim, but it's true, both figuratively and literally.

I've Got This Friend Who... is the result of more than a century of work by the leading national children's crisis charity KidsPeace, its current 2,000 doctors and child care professionals, child and adolescent development experts from Harvard Medical School and Brown University, and—most important—more than half a million of America's teens, who are firsthand authorities on the biggest problems kids face growing up today.

Together, they have created a unique how-to manual to help teens and their friends survive the often challenging and sometimes perilous adolescent years. Written in the voice of today's young people, *I've Got This Friend Who...* was designed to help kids at exactly the critical points in their lives when they are usually least likely to turn to adults for help. Since young people's peers know just about as much as they do, this can often lead them into trouble that could have been avoided if only they—or a friend—had a little more information about how to handle things.

That's where this book comes in. The topics, information, and coping techniques featured here are based on expert knowledge and the firsthand experiences of thousands of actual teens, obtained through an innovative, problem-solving resource designed to help young people work out stresses and problems before they become overwhelming. This resource—TeenCentral.Net—was created in 1998 by Harvard Medical School's Dr. Alvin Poussaint, Brown University Child Study Center founder Dr. Lewis P. Lipsitt, and KidsPeace Executive Vice President Joseph A. Vallone, all cofounders with Lee Salk's brother, polio vaccine pioneer Jonas Salk, of the KidsPeace Lee Salk Center for Research.

Providing anonymous and free 24/7 counseling, TeenCentral.Net receives more than two million hits each month from teens with diverse backgrounds in all fifty states, military bases around the world, and one hundred foreign countries. Powered by innovative software that guides kids through a process of problem identification, information sharing, and crisis-resolution techniques, the site has become an ever-expanding database of real stories, revealing what's actually happening to our kids, what they're feeling, what the critical trends and hot-button issues are, and what they're doing about them. The chapter topics and the voices of *I've Got This Friend Who...* are based on an in-depth analysis of that database of more than 500,000 stories. Accompanied by sensible, easy-to-use information from child care specialists, this is essentially a book *for America's teens by America's teens.*

There has perhaps never been a better time for this type of tool for teens. Today's kids face a range of pressures and dangers in the world that would have been unimaginable just a generation ago—from waves of dangerously accessible new drugs, alarmingly high rates of child abuse, and single-parent homes, to cyber-bullying, school shootings, and terrorism. But even the age-old challenges most kids have faced growing up need new solutions.

Since its founding in Bethlehem, Pennsylvania, in 1882, KidsPeace, the National Center for Kids Overcoming Crisis, has been working to develop new ideas, programs, and practical strategies to help millions of children and families avoid and overcome the kinds of crises that can strike any child. While we have directly touched the lives of thousands of children, this project aims for the first time to harness the accumulated wisdom of 125 years of hope, help, and healing in the child crisis field; cutting-edge research and theory from the KidsPeace Lee Salk Center for Research; and the cumulative experience—and, yes, savvy—of America's youth.

This book is the culmination of 125 years of experience and cumulative wisdom. KidsPeace will ensure that it makes its way into the hands of as many young people as possible, so it can be a bulwark against danger, ignorance, uncertainty, and destructive choices—and perhaps a new road map that, in a turbulent world, will help give kids peace.

C.T. O'Donnell II
President and Chief Executive Officer
KidsPeace

Lorrie Henderson, PH.D., L.C.S.W.
Chief Operating Officer
KidsPeace

Joseph A. Vallone, C.F.R.E.
Executive Vice President
KidsPeace

Herbert Mandell, M.D.
National Medical Director
KidsPeace

Alvin Poussaint, M.D.
Professor of Psychiatry
Harvard Medical School
National Director
KidsPeace Lee Salk Center
   for Research

Lewis P. Lipsitt, PH.D.
Professor Emeritus
Brown University
National Director
KidsPeace Lee Salk Center
   for Research

ACKNOWLEDGMENTS

THIS BOOK IS A PRODUCT of the intellectual wisdom, professional knowledge, expert contributions, and hard work of a large group of individuals from within and from outside KidsPeace, who came together to create a work that speaks directly to kids about the problems they face growing up. We wish to extend our warmest gratitude to the many content contributors, whose biographies are included at the end of the book. We also wish to recognize the tremendous efforts of KidsPeace's National Director of Public Education, Anna Radev, who was the project editor of this work. Her countless hours of directing, writing, and editing have provided a single voice for these numerous contributors, and her unique idea resulted in the "dialogue format." In addition, we also wish to recognize a number of other KidsPeace contributors who lent their time and efforts in various other ways to ensure the success of this project. They include Caren Chaffee, Director of Government Relations; Dolly Cary, Assistant to the Executive Vice President of Strategic Advancement; Pat Sullivan, Senior Writer; Susan Kauffman, Administrative Support Manager; Lauren Kronisch, Communications Associate; and Cindy Traupman, Assistant to the President.

Sincerest thanks to all for your hard work!

INTRODUCTION

EVERY DAY YOU WALK OUT OF YOUR HOUSE, close the door behind you, and step into a world full of hope, promise, and opportunity. As a teenager, you encounter a world of endless possibilities. But you are also walking out into the unknown, and with it comes risk and uncertainty. On any given day, you may face first-time decisions, nail-biting problems, or crushing disappointments. You may struggle to do the right thing or just to get through the day and make it a few steps further in your journey of life.

Every day for 125 years, KidsPeace, the National Center for Kids Overcoming Crisis, has been keeping watch and working to bring hope, help, and healing to children, giving them tools to overcome the challenges of growing up. Over the years, KidsPeace has gathered a great deal of knowledge and expertise on children's issues, as well as unique insights on how to empower them to make each day a victory. With its sixty-five centers nationwide, more than 2,500 employees, and countless supporters, KidsPeace has directly touched the lives of 150,000 children and reached into the homes of millions more through public education and prevention.

Kids often feel they're powerless to deal with many of the problems out there, and a lot of adults reinforce that perception. But the truth is that all young people have the inner strength and ability to have a say in their lives and a choice when it comes to the trials before them. This book was written to help you find your inner courage and character and gain a sense of control over your destiny, despite problems, by making good choices and reaching out to trustworthy adults. The same goes for your friends, and you can definitely give them a helping hand along the way.

This book is based on the trials and tribulations of thousands of teens. The concerns they expressed are recounted here through discussions among six fictitious kids who come together to talk about their biggest worries. Each chapter explores a different topic. These topics were the most frequently selected issues of concern by kids who logged on to TeenCentral.Net in 2005, and they are the topics that seem to be the most interesting or troublesome to older kids and teens today. The six kids featured in this book have very different backgrounds, ages, personalities, and points of view. Imagine sitting in a room with five of your own schoolmates, who are very different from you, and talking about these various issues. Which one of these kids would you be?

The Kids

Karen Karen is sixteen. She always plays the devil's advocate. She is very smart, outspoken, independent, eccentric, and nonconformist. She likes to march to her own drum and is unconventional in her style, interests, and ideas. She is not part of the "in crowd" but has plenty of friends, and she isn't preoccupied with being popular. She is comfortable in her own skin, and she gets that just because "everyone else is doing it" doesn't mean she has to. But she is also curious about many things and life experiences—she's the kind who might try anything once to see what it's like—so she is tempted to explore the unknown. Her dilemma isn't peer pressure or the opinions of others, but rather her own curious, explorative nature. So she is the one who asks the "why" or the "why not" questions and needs to be convinced if/why something is bad by making the argument.

Ryan Ryan is seventeen. He is a bit of a maverick. He is on the basketball and swim teams and could be considered one of the "popular" kids, but he is also in the student government and the drama club. So although he is liked, has many friends, and does find himself in situations where other kids are doing "bad" things, he is not the quintessential "jock" who applauds and goes along for the ride. He has a levelheadedness when it comes to various issues that others his age might consider "cool." He is a voice of reason and is a good "positive peer pressure" role model, as he can use his popularity to enforce good practices and habits among his peers.

Eric Eric is fifteen. He is the class "nerd." He is very well schooled and informed about most subjects. Of course, he has had his share of being shunned or alienated, especially by the "popular" kids, for not being "cool," for sticking to his guns, and for not going along with the crowd. Although he covers it up fairly well, he has his angst about not fitting in, not being invited to all the parties, and not dating much. But he's made some choices about who he wants to be, and he is sticking to them. He has had plenty of free time to read and better himself, so he has read up extensively on things and knows what the consequences and repercussions of bad choices can be. He knows where he's going in life.

Ashley Ashley is thirteen. She has just gotten to high school and is unsure of herself. She has a good upbringing and good moral values, but she also desperately wants to fit in and be accepted. She isn't sure how to go about it—which values are worth compromising and which are not—and she feels confused and pressured. She's also a perfectionist, which is making things even harder. She has found herself in certain situations she didn't know how to handle and is on the edge of a slippery slope. She can see and empathize with the argument for why people *do* engage in certain behaviors—she understands the appealing, enticing, "beneficial" side of these behaviors that makes them so hard to resist and easy to fall into. She needs direction to understand more clearly that although some types of behavior may be appealing at certain times, they come at a very high price.

Emile Emile is eighteen. He comes from a troubled family background and a tough neighborhood. In his teens, Emile went through a rebellious period that lasted several years when he engaged in nearly every conceivable "bad" behavior out there. In the last year, he decided to straighten out and sought help. Now he describes himself as a survivor who's on the right track, although his earlier actions have left scars and challenges that he struggles with every day. He's a senior, finishing his high-school education and planning ahead. As someone who has "been through the fire and back," he is an eye-opener for the others. He reveals to them the truth behind many of the myths they may have heard, sharing his real-world experiences and those of people he knew in his old neighborhood. He provides perspective and a reality check that bring things into focus when issues and arguments seem fuzzy.

Jessica Jessica is seventeen. She is very popular, a cheerleader, and she likes to have a good time. She thinks she is young and free and should enjoy herself as much as she can. She goes along with whatever her "crew" has in mind to have a good time. She doesn't think she is doing anything to the extent that it will become a problem. She is a "recreational abuser" of various types of rebellious teen behaviors and is in denial that these things will build up to anything serious. She doesn't quite see what's so bad about experimenting with certain things in moderation every now and then. She thinks she is in control of it all and knows exactly what she is doing.

Regardless of which kid you identify with most, we hope this book will help you make informed, smart decisions that will keep you safe, healthy, and happy—and also allow you to help a friend in need. A safe journey through life is what we all want for ourselves and our friends, and it shouldn't be left to chance.

I'VE GOT THIS FRIEND WHO...

One difficult choice kids and teens struggle with every day is whether or not to drink alcohol. Alcohol is a constant temptation, and the pressure is great. Drinking has always carried an image of being "cool." Television and magazine ads bombard kids with images that tell them alcohol makes them seem more mature, fashionable, desirable, and fun. Also, the growing prevalence of much more serious, dangerous, and deadly drugs on the market makes alcohol look mild and almost harmless in comparison.

—Janet Sterba, L.P.C.

But the problems that come with drinking are still very real and sometimes deadly. Alcohol can disrupt kids' physical and emotional health, and it can interfere with their ability to get by in the world. At best, it takes away a person's ability to make good judgments. When you are not in control of yourself and your actions, it can lead to a whole range of other bad choices and bigger problems. In the worst-case scenario, it can cost kids their lives. It happens all too often.

—Nirmala Yarra Karna, M.D.

Ryan

TOASTING THE TOWN

Lifting Your Spirits with Alcohol Can Lead to Head-On Collisions That Can Shatter Your Life

Jessica   Eric   Karen   Emile   Ashley

Alcohol *So What about It?*

Karen Drinking alcohol—what's the big deal? Some kids drink once in a while, some do nothing but party, and other kids never touch the stuff. It's a matter of personal choice, and we all have to make the decision for ourselves. Sounds easy enough—a clear choice between drinking or not drinking—right? Well, in reality, it isn't that simple or clear. Alcohol has its appeal—I mean, it makes you feel and act differently for sure, and sometimes that's exactly what you want. Then, there's also a lot of pressure at our age—to make friends, be accepted and belong, be liked, and fit in. Peer pressure is a major part of being a kid, and the right answer isn't always clear. On top of that, people we idolize and look up to often glamorize alcohol and encourage us to "get with it." So where do we start?

Eric Well, I think we start by talking about what drinking alcohol is all about. Basically, *alcohol* is a colorless, unstable, flammable liquid that is

Alcohol
a colorless, unstable, flammable liquid made by fermenting sugars and starches

Types of Drinking	
Abstaining	Not drinking at all, or one or two drinks a year
Infrequent drinking	One drink or less a month
Light drinking	Two to four drinks once a month, or one drink three to four times a month
Moderate drinking	One drink once a week, or two to six drinks three to four times a month, or five or more drinks once a month
Moderately heavy drinking	Two to four drinks once a week, or more drinks three to four times a month
Heavy drinking	Five or more drinks at least once a week

made by fermenting sugars and starches. A lot of beverages contain alcohol, and many people drink it. There are several types of drinking (see above).

Ashley What about *social drinking*? People use that term a lot.

Social drinking
having one or two drinks when out with friends

Eric Well, when adults say "social drinking," it generally means having a drink or two now and then when you are out with friends. Usually social drinkers are light drinkers. But with people our age, drinking is different and often gets out of control when it's part of hanging out. A lot of kids end up drinking a lot when they're around other people who drink. So, if you are often around kids who drink a lot, you might become a heavy social drinker and not even know how it happened.

Ryan Yeah, I agree with Eric. I mean, if you think about it, most adults don't spend even half as much time as kids do hanging out and socializing with friends. They're too busy with work, kids, groceries, laundry, and other stuff. But hanging out is one of the main things we kids do—sometimes every day and all day. Also, I don't think drinking is as seductive for adults, because they're allowed to do it. But it's like the forbidden apple to us, since we're not allowed to drink before we are twenty-one.

Ashley I've heard "binge drinking" a lot too. That's, like, when you chug a whole bunch of alcohol really quickly, right? Like, what people do at keg parties in college? My sister's in a sorority...

Binging
drinking five or more drinks one after the other in a very short time

Emile Yeah, *binging* is when you drink five or more drinks one after the other in a very short time. People do it through games like funneling, chugging, or "keg stand" at parties.

Eric And what happens is, when you drink that much that fast, the alcohol in your blood jumps up to a high level very quickly. That level is your *blood alcohol concentration (BAC)* or *blood alcohol level (BAL)*. Just to be clear, a regular drink is one twelve-ounce bottle of beer or wine cooler, one five-ounce glass of wine, or a shot (1.5 ounces) of hard liquor, like whiskey. How much alcohol it takes and how quickly you have to drink it to get tipsy or drunk depends on how tall you are, how much you weigh, what shape you're in, if you ate while drinking, how much sleep you've had, if you're taking medication, your body chemistry and your tolerance to alcohol, your mood, and your age.

Ashley Wow, I didn't know some of that. So, like, the bigger and heavier you are, the more alcohol it takes to make you drunk? And being tired or having an empty stomach makes it, like, easier to feel drunk too?

Eric Yeah. Say you weigh 200 pounds. It would take two times more alcohol to get to the same BAL than if you weighed 100 pounds. That's why some people feel drunk after a glass of wine and others can have three beers and not be drunk. The legal BAL for driving after drinking in the United States is 0.08 percent, by the way, which basically means up to two drinks. But that also depends on your weight, tolerance, and the other stuff.

Ashley So, what about, like, medication—what does that have to do with anything?

Ryan Basically, alcohol is a drug and a *depressant,* Ash. What that means is, at first, it gives you a high. But after a while, it starts to slow you down, slows your movements and reactions, makes you tired and sleepy, and even sad or depressed. Well, some medications do the same thing—even some over-the-counter stuff. So you have to be very careful about mixing them with alcohol, because they will have a double impact and will make your blood pressure drop way low. You could die. And other meds just have bad effects when you combine them with alcohol—they can make you feel weird, sick, or dizzy.

Emile All right, something else we should talk about is alcoholism. Alcohol, just like drugs, is *addictive,* meaning you can get hooked on it. *Alcoholism* is a disorder where a person drinks a lot and is dependent on alcohol—physically, mentally, or both. That means your body or your mind or both crave it really often. And it affects how you get by in the world—socially, at work, at home, everywhere. It's also called *alcohol abuse* and *alcohol dependence.*

Eric Now here are some facts about alcohol and kids ages twelve to seventeen: 7.2 million drank at least once in the past year; 2.7 million

Blood alcohol concentration
the level of alcohol in your blood after you've been drinking

Depressant
a substance that slows your movements and reactions, makes you tired, and may cause you to feel sad or depressed

Alcoholism
a disorder in which a person drinks a lot and is physically and/or mentally dependent on alcohol

drank once a month or more in the past year; 1 million drank at least once a week in the last year; girls are as likely as boys their age to drink; Hispanics were as likely as white non-Hispanics to be drinkers; and African American kids were least likely to be current drinkers.[1]

Also, girls are binging more, while boys are binging less than they used to. The punch line: Every day, 5,400 young people under sixteen take their first drink of alcohol.[2] And there's more stuff that will blow your mind.

Karen Here's what I found. Eighty to 90 percent of middle school kids don't drink. But the numbers go up sharply for eighth- to twelfth-graders.

Emile Yeah, and binge drinking is very common for kids who drink because it's hard to just have one when everyone else keeps going, and the momentum is building in your group.

Ninety-Nine Bottles of Beer on the Wall...
Why Booze?

Eric So, a lot of kids drink, but plenty of kids don't.

Jessica Yeah, who's that, Eric? Kids like you, who stay home buried in books all the time?

Statistics Speak for Themselves
‣ More than 50 percent of all students in grades six to twelve in 2004 had tried alcohol, including beer, wine coolers, or hard liquor.[3]
‣ Of the young people who drink, almost 7.2 million (19 percent) are binge drinkers and 2.3 million (6 percent) are heavy drinkers.[4] Kids usually have their first drink around age twelve.[5]
‣ The average age at which kids begin drinking regularly is 15.9 years old.[6]
‣ Sixty-five percent of kids who drink get alcohol from friends or family.
‣ Children who begin drinking before age fifteen are four times more likely to become alcoholics as adults than kids who begin drinking at twenty-one, the legal drinking age.[7]
‣ Alcohol-related fatality rates are almost two times greater for eighteen-, nineteen-, and twenty-year-olds as for people over twenty-one. More than 40 percent of crash fatalities among eighteen-, nineteen-, and twenty-year-olds are alcohol related.[8]
‣ Teenagers make up less than 7 percent of the nation's licensed drivers, but they are involved in 15 percent of all fatal crashes.[9]

Alcohol Drinking among Eighth-Graders through Twelfth-Graders

Action	Eighth-Graders	Tenth-Graders	Twelfth-Graders
Drank in the past month	25%	40%	53%
Got drunk	8%	22%	34%
Binged in the past two weeks	15%	25%	30%
Drank every day	1%	2%	4%

2004 statistics[10]

Karen Okay, so why *do* kids drink?

Jessica Well, because it seems like everybody drinks. I mean, I don't know anyone who doesn't—my parents, all my relatives, my friends. Every time I go to, like, a get-together, or out to dinner with family friends, or to a friend's house, or just sit around with some of my older cousins, they all drink. Even, like, the minister at church drinks, and of course, there's wine for communion. Alcohol is common in many homes. And let's face it—parties, picnics, wedding receptions, whatever—if adults, like, get together to have a good time, alcohol is always in the mix. Adults tell us not to drink, but their example says the opposite.

Let's be fair—drinking is legal, so it's not like drugs where you're breaking the law. The bottom line: I've been around alcohol all my life, so what I know is, it can't be, like, all that bad, right?

Ryan Wrong. Let's set the record straight: Just because adults drink doesn't mean it's okay for you to. Drinking before you're twenty-one— that *is* illegal, and you *are* breaking the law. Actually, Jess, not everyone drinks, and neither do all adults. It really depends on what company you keep. In some homes, it is done, in others, not so much. About 36 percent of adults don't drink at all. I happen to know a lot of people like that—like my parents and many of my relatives, some of my neighbors, and even Coach Shepard. Surprised?

Eric As far as parents and other adults we admire go—yeah, we do look up to them, hoping to find answers to a lot of stuff. When our parents drink, and especially if they drink a lot, we think since they do it, why not me? And we end up "doing as they do, not as they say." But you also have to think about it, you guys—adults are people too, and they can make mistakes just like kids do.

Karen Yeah, my Uncle Mike was like that. I loved him, but he wasn't someone I'd want to be like when I grow up.

Jessica   Okay, I'm pretty sure all of us here have had a drink before, except maybe Eric. I admit, I drink when I'm out with my friends, and you all know, it really does, like, make a difference in your mood and how you feel—how much fun you have. Alcohol helps you relax, loosen up, and be more talkative, bubbly, funny, and spontaneous, and, yeah, silly too, which is, like, the whole point. Besides, how stupid would it be if I'm chilling with my friends and alcohol gets passed around and I am like, "Ehhh, no, thank you!"

Ashley   Yeah, I mean it's hard when pretty much everyone who's anyone drinks. If people like that do notice you and invite you somewhere, you pretty much have to be cool and, like, go along to get along. If they end up thinking you are boring and stupid and immature, they definitely won't invite you again, and you'll go back to being a nobody just like that.

Ryan   So, let me get this. You're saying drinking solely for the sake of other people's opinion of you and to make them like you so you can be popular is worth it? Nice way to be an adult, Ash. News flash: Drinking doesn't make you mature. Standing up for yourself and being your own person does. People can lead you down many bad paths if you don't learn to think for yourself.

Ashley   But it's really tough when you're trying to fit in and make a good impression on a bunch of kids who are, like, way older and cooler. If alcohol calms your nerves and helps you loosen up, it can make a big difference.

Ryan   Ash, we get it. But if it really is that important to you, there are other ways to deal with nervousness. Alcohol is not the only choice or the best one. You can go with someone else to give each other strength, you can ease into talking with other people, you can even do some breathing techniques to help you relax.

Jessica   Okay, well, that's all good—I can, like, somehow avoid drinking in high school without my social life becoming a complete disaster. But then comes college. You have to learn sometime, because how do you avoid drinking in college?

Karen   We're talking about alcohol here, not badminton. No college awards a degree in drunkenness or lewd behavior, and I'm pretty sure that's unlikely to change. Yes, a lot of college students do drink, but from what I hear, many of those situations don't end too well.

Why Do Kids Drink?

> Out of curiosity—experimentation to discover what it feels like and what effect it has

> Peer pressure to fit in and be accepted by other kids who drink

> To appear cool, mature, grown up, adventurous, fun, and knowledgeable about adult behavior

> To forget about or escape from everyday problems or a life crisis

> To rebel against adults or imposed norms and to assert independence

> To feel better, happier, and livelier

> To ease nervousness and become more outgoing and likable

> To medicate emotional problems or symptoms like depression, anxiety, fears, or stress

> Because they believe everybody drinks and drinking is a normal part of life and socializing

> Because alcohol is easily available to them in their homes or other places

> Because people they look up to—parents, siblings, relatives, authority figures, celebrities —drink and set that example for them, or tolerate or encourage the behavior

> For the thrill of it

Emile Jess, when I listen to you, I can totally hear myself a few years back. I thought the more I drank, the more cool and fun I became, and the more people liked me. People think it makes other people look up to them, because they seem grown up and mature. Or you drink to show you'll do what you want—make your own rules and stick it to the people who are telling you what to do. And sometimes, you just want to cut loose or feel better. When you have enough drinks, everything stops mattering, and it's all good. It helps make bad things go away, and that's why so many people I know drank and still do. That's why I drank. And take it from me—it was a bad idea. Liquor's a false god.

Jessica Well, I mean, yeah, drinking a lot all the time is probably a bad idea, just like overdoing anything is usually bad for you. My dad always says moderation is the key. That's what I'm saying. Having, like, one or two drinks—I just don't see how that's so horrible.

Eric Okay, well, even assuming you can keep your drinking from getting out of hand, that's not the only issue. How about drunk driving and the accidents that happen all the time when kids *DUI—drive under the influence* —or get in cars with people who do? You don't have to be an alcoholic or a binge-drinker—it only takes a couple of drinks and one time of drunk driving to get into some real trouble.

Jessica Again, the word *drunk*. I am not saying drive drunk. Absolutely not, of course! But there's, like, a difference between having a couple of drinks and being drunk. When I have a drink or two, I don't feel drunk, and it doesn't affect my ability to drive. If anything, it makes me even more careful—I pay, like, even closer attention to other drivers. If I do feel like the alcohol is getting to me, I have a coffee or two to clear my head and wait it out. If I actually feel *drunk,* then I just don't get behind the wheel. On top of that, I don't know anyone who's had some drinks and then gotten into an accident.

Ryan Ahhh, yes, the "it's not going to happen to me" attitude! I know it well.

Myths about Alcohol
❯ Alcohol is legal, so it's not that big a deal to drink.
❯ Popular kids, good athletes, and even good students drink, so it's okay for me to drink.
❯ Saying "no" will make me look immature, uncool, and unadventurous. Everybody will think I'm a loser or dork, and no one will want to hang out with me.
❯ Everybody in college drinks, so if I don't learn to drink, I will be left out.
❯ My parents and all the other adults I know drink and keep alcohol in the house, so they must be okay with me drinking.
❯ If my favorite celebrities drink, why shouldn't I?
❯ The more I drink, the happier, more outgoing, and fun I become and the more people like me.
❯ Binge drinking is no big deal—I'm just having a little fun. Nothing bad will happen.
❯ I am not an alcoholic unless I drink a lot every single day.
❯ I drink because I want to, not because I need to. I can stop anytime.
❯ Even if I've had some drinks, if I don't feel drunk, I am okay to drive.
❯ I drive better when I've been drinking because I am more cautious and vigilant.
❯ It's okay to get into a car with someone who's been drinking if they don't look drunk.
❯ If I've been drinking and have to drive, a strong cup of coffee will sober me up.
❯ I know what I am doing, and I am completely in control even when I've had several drinks, so nobody can take advantage of me.
❯ An accident won't happen to me.

Karen Everything we're saying here makes sense, but I get why it's so hard to choose. I mean, it might seem obvious what the right choice is, but then we get mixed messages not only from our friends and families but also from society. I mean, every day we are bombarded by images on TV, in movies, on billboards, in magazines, and in video clips that make alcohol look so cool and natural. Alcohol was shown in more than 90 percent of the 200 most popular movie rentals for 1996 and 1997 and in 17 percent of the 1,000 most popular songs, including almost half of all the rap music recording.[11] How do you say "no"?

Eric Well, for one thing, we can all learn to think for ourselves. You can't agree with everything out there without question. The advertising, it's there for a reason—to sell a product. So, those people are looking out for what they want, and it's about making money. But what the media doesn't show is the dark side of drinking—all the bad stuff. An important part of growing up is learning to make choices for yourself and figuring out the right ones. Underage drinking isn't one of them.

Take One Down, Pass It Around...
Who's at Risk for Drinking?

Karen Anyone can get tempted into alcohol. The younger you are, the more impressionable you are. You look up to older people to be an example for you.

Ryan What adds to the problem is how easy it is to get booze nowadays. Plenty of grown-ups are willing to buy alcohol for underage kids because they think it's a rite of passage or no big thing. Some parents even have drinking parties to keep their kids from drinking and driving, or to "teach kids how to drink the right way."

Emile That's pretty messed up, because kids who start drinking before age fifteen are four times more likely to become alcoholics than kids who don't.

A Losing Game of Spin the Bottle
The Consequences of Drinking

Karen Wanting to forget your problems or to be accepted by others is totally normal. Everyone feels that need during their life, especially teens. We all want to be liked—nobody wants to be alone. And we all have things in our lives we want to forget.

Choosing not to drink can mean missing out on a lot—the experience itself, fitting in, the group closeness, being seen as cool or grown up. And there isn't a huge neon warning sign with flashing lights right in front of you whenever the temptation comes up. So, unless you have all the facts and you can see through the myths, deciding to drink or not can be very confusing. No wonder so many kids give in. But it's a temporary fix, and its feel-good side doesn't make up for all the problems. Before you decide to listen to that little voice in your head that says, "Maybe I should try it—it's not like it'll kill me," listen to these facts Eric and I found. Here are a whole lot of reasons you should pass.

Eric Alcohol is a drug, even though it is a legal drug. And it's not legal for anyone under twenty-one. So you can get into trouble if you're caught. A criminal record isn't exactly the best way to a bright future. It can affect getting into the colleges you want, getting into the military, finding job opportunities, and even getting your driver's license. What a drag.

Alcohol also has a bunch of bad side effects, right after you drink and way later—loss of balance or coordination, blurred vision, slurred speech, trouble moving around, dizziness, stumbling, and tripping—just to start. These don't exactly make you the poster child for coolness and having it together. You actually look stupid and out of control, but that's the least of your problems.

Karen Some more serious side effects of drinking are blackouts, digestive problems, liver damage, central nervous system and heart problems, mouth and throat cancers, and even problems with intimacy or being able to have kids one day. *Blackouts* are moments when you don't have any memory of what happened or what you did. They happen when you have way too much to drink really fast and can last just a few minutes, sometimes hours, or even days. The scary part is, because people don't pass out during a blackout, they can walk, talk, and continue to drink like everything's normal, so no one else even knows it's happening.

The more you drink, the more damage to your body. Depending on how much and how often, drinking can shorten your life more than ten years!

Eric And as Ryan said before, alcohol is a depressant. When you first drink, you get happy and euphoric. But when you come off your "high," the alcohol begins to act as a downer. The more you drink, the more your mental and physical functions slow down. You start feeling sad and depressed, you want to sleep, or in the worst case, you pass out or go into a coma. Abusing alcohol for a long time can also cause brain damage.

What it comes down to is booze affects your mind, feelings, and actions. It takes away your control of a situation because you can't think straight or make smart choices. It makes you reckless or vulnerable and an easy target. It lowers your inhibitions and makes you do risky things—like getting into fights, having unprotected sex, accidentally hurting yourself or others, or worst of all, getting behind the wheel. People always think, "That won't happen to me," but alcohol affects that.

Every year, 870,000 girls ages fifteen to nineteen have unwanted pregnancies, and alcohol is usually involved. And did you know that the three leading causes of death for fifteen- to twenty-four-year-olds are homicide, suicide, and car crashes[12]—and that alcohol plays the biggest part in them? If alcohol is in the picture, you're also much more likely to suffer from depression or to get raped or arrested.

Ryan Also, we tease and make fun of people when they drink way too much and can't stand up, walk, talk without slurring, or remember what they did. But binge drinking is no joke. It can cause a *hangover* the next day—feeling sick, feeling dizzy, having a horrible headache, being very sensitive to light and sounds, just basically being useless. Binging can also cause blackouts, so you won't remember if you did anything risky or if you hurt yourself—by falling, cutting yourself, spraining an ankle, getting hit by a car—or hurt someone else.

But the worst that can happen is *alcohol poisoning*—drinking so much that it makes you pass out, causes brain damage, or even kills you. The level of alcohol in your blood is so high that your body goes into shock. About 4,500 young people die of alcohol poisoning every year.[13]

Emile Then, there's addiction. More than ten million people around the country are slaves to alcohol, and three million are under twenty years old.[14]

Do you want a real shocker? I am a recovering alcoholic. Surprised? Alcoholism is a very real and serious illness that can make it difficult to live a normal life. There are many different types of alcoholics—daily drinkers, bingers, and even functional drinkers. But they are all physically, mentally, and/or emotionally dependent on alcohol. I was. It screws up your whole life. You have a hard time keeping a job, making and keeping friends, achieving your goals in life, or even doing simple things that others take for granted, like stopping after one or two drinks. Everything else stops mattering.

Jessica Jeez, Em! How'd it get that bad?

Emile It's easier than you think. I was going through all this stuff, and I thought I'd found a cure for my problems and a best friend. Before I knew it, alcohol became my *only* friend. It seems under control at first, slowly creeping into your life until it takes over. You think drinking is okay as long as you don't do it all the time. You convince yourself that "having a couple of drinks" doesn't make you an "alkie." That's what my so-called friends used to say. Then, you start drinking every day, but again, you say to yourself, "No big deal. I drink because I want to, not because I have to. I can stop anytime I want." And then, before you know it, it has a hold on you and you can't stop. You need it—you have to

Hangover
headache, dizziness, light and sound sensitivity, and general illness that occurs the next day after drinking

Alcohol poisoning
drinking so much that your body goes into shock, you pass out, and you may experience brain damage or die

have it. You think about it really often, and it affects the person you are and the way you act until you become completely unable to function. I thought I was the man—that I had it under control. Yeah, right! Doesn't sound like much fun, eh?

Karen And the whole thing about college and how drinking affects your experience? Just listen to this. About 1,400 college students eighteen to twenty-four years old die every year from alcohol-related incidents, including car crashes. Another 500,000 are hurt after drinking, and close to 600,000 get assaulted by another student who has been drinking. More than 70,000 students are sexually hurt or raped in alcohol-related incidents, and 100,000 get too drunk to remember if they agreed to have sex

Consequences for Specific Stages of Drinking		
Alcohol Use	**Short-Term Effects**	**Long-Term Repercussions**
Social drinking	❯ Mild high (buzz) ❯ Feeling a false sense of happiness or contentment ❯ Feeling unlike yourself ❯ Mild dizziness ❯ Mild hangover the next day	❯ Drinking without parental knowledge multiple times ❯ First intoxication (drunk) ❯ Opening the door to further drinking
Occasional binge drinking	❯ Poor judgment ❯ Loss of inhibitions ❯ Poor balance or coordination ❯ Forgetting what happened ❯ Reduced school performance ❯ School suspension ❯ Avoidance of teachers ❯ Sneaking out ❯ Vague explanations or outright lies to parents and friends ❯ Spending time and energy planning next use ❯ Distorted senses, such as hearing and sight ❯ Bad breath ❯ Stronger emotions ❯ Severe and unexplained mood swings ❯ Dizziness ❯ Vomiting ❯ Complete loss of consciousness ❯ Alcohol poisoning and feeling really sick	❯ Being argumentative or aggressive ❯ Acting out ❯ Getting into fights ❯ Hurting yourself or others ❯ Having your first clash with the law ❯ Having unprotected sex ❯ Blackouts ❯ Involvement with psychiatrist and/or psychologist ❯ Minimizing and/or denying there is a problem ❯ Liver damage ❯ Mild brain damage ❯ Memory loss ❯ Internal bleeding ❯ Impotence ❯ Suicidal ideations ❯ Becoming a victim of assault or sexual assault ❯ Alcohol poisoning leading to coma or death

continued on next page

I've Got This Friend Who...

Consequences for Specific Stages of Drinking (continued)

Alcohol Use	Short-Term Effects	Long-Term Repercussions
Regular alcohol use	‣ Big changes in attitude, mood, or behavior ‣ Loss of typical interests ‣ Carrying alcohol to school ‣ Money problems ‣ Withdrawing to your room with door closed ‣ Abusing others verbally and physically ‣ Avoiding friends who don't drink ‣ Thinking about alcohol often ‣ Acting out ‣ Shoplifting ‣ Vandalizing ‣ Running away ‣ Driving under the influence ‣ Failing in school ‣ Lying often to family and friends ‣ Injuries ‣ Weight loss ‣ Bad hygiene ‣ More frequent blackouts ‣ Shorter attention span ‣ Depression ‣ Feelings of inferiority ‣ Shame and guilt ‣ Possibly combining drugs with alcohol ‣ Feeling depressed or out of control	‣ Buildup of negative consequences ‣ Loss of longtime friends ‣ Expulsion from school ‣ Drinking and driving regularly ‣ Committing murder or suicide ‣ Regular blackouts ‣ Increased violent behaviors ‣ Increased criminal behavior ‣ Physical problems ‣ Increased or decreased weight ‣ Memory problems ‣ Increasing drug use ‣ Less concern with own safety ‣ More serious negative effects on the liver, kidneys, and brain
Addiction/ alcoholism	‣ Not caring about how other people feel ‣ Disregarding own life or future for alcohol ‣ Putting drinking before anything else ‣ Committing crimes ‣ Using alcohol daily ‣ Getting fired or expelled ‣ Staying away from home ‣ Losing touch with important people ‣ Having unprotected sex all the time ‣ Extreme mood swings ‣ Complete loss of normal interests ‣ Severe depression ‣ Developing psychotic symptoms ‣ Not being able to function daily	‣ High risk for HIV, hepatitis C, and other sexually transmitted diseases (STDs) ‣ Constantly in trouble with the law ‣ Frequent jail time ‣ Suspended driver's license ‣ Severed ties with all loved ones (friends and family) ‣ Severe brain abnormalities and mental problems (like depression, paranoia, or psychoses like schizophrenia) ‣ Psychiatric hospitalization ‣ Living on the street ‣ Being badly hurt or killed while living on the street ‣ Severe damage to liver and kidneys ‣ Suicide attempts ‣ Death

or not. About 400,000 college kids have unprotected sex after drinking,[15] and that can lead to unwanted pregnancies or *sexually transmitted diseases (STDs)*. How is that for truth or dare?

Ryan Drinking also gives you a false high—a sense of being invincible that can be very costly. You become careless, thinking you can do everything better when you drink, including drive. You get into a car, and then you can become the scariest statistic of all—an alcohol-related death.

And even if you don't intend to drive drunk, it doesn't matter, because alcohol also makes it hard for you to judge if someone else has had too many. If you're drinking too, you can't make the call if they are too drunk to drive. Alcohol dulls your senses and keeps you from taking the danger seriously.

Driving drunk happens a lot. Every day, kids get into cars after having a few, or with someone who's been drinking, and become victims of a bad choice. Sure, you could get lucky and walk away with a few scrapes and bruises. Nearly 2,000 kids every year aren't so lucky, though, and their drunken joyride becomes their last.

And if it happened to you, it wouldn't be just you paying the price. Your parents, relatives, friends, and everybody who cares about you will suffer the consequences. Many families and communities across the country live with that pain and loss every day. Ask yourself if you want to become the next statistic—or have your best friend, girlfriend, boyfriend, brother, or sister become one. One kid is one too many. I know— four years ago, my brother became a statistic.

Jessica God, Ryan! I never knew that! I'm so sorry! That's why you're so anti-this-stuff! No wonder I've never seen you drink at any party. Not even the prom. I am so sorry. I feel so stupid.

Ryan You know what really gets me? Every time, I think, what a waste. My brother was an awesome guy, a good student—everybody thought the world of him. Great football player—the best. Had three different colleges fighting over him with full scholarships. And then, one night, he makes one bad decision, and just like that, it's all over. For nothing—of all the stupid ways to end it! Now, all I have are my memories, and the more time that goes by, the more of him I forget. I'm so scared that one day, all I'll remember of him is that stupid, horrible night. I don't want anybody else to go through what my family went through when we got that call.

Eric I remember when your brother's accident happened. My mom works in the ER. She told me they brought in some kids that were in a horrible crash. I recognized your brother's name right away. Sorry your family had to go through that—must have been really hard.

Karen Ryan, thanks for opening up. If it can help one of us here think differently, it's definitely worth it.

Ryan Thanks, guys. Just wanted you to know it's not just numbers and statistics. It *is* real lives.

Seeing the Empty Glass as Half Full
Coping with or Covering Up Your Drinking

Karen Okay, so a lot of kids do end up drinking, but do we know which ones?

Jessica Yeah, I mean, everybody more or less knows. A couple of parties and pretty much everyone knows who's game and who's not.

Ryan Do they? Sometimes you know, but not always. Some kids actually *don't* want people to know, especially if their drinking is a problem. They might be trying to deny it's out of control—especially if a friend or loved one doesn't approve of it. Then there's a lot of pressure to hide it.

Emile Yeah. And obviously, the kids who have been doing it a long time and don't want other people to know become pros at keeping people from finding out. They are secretive, really good at lying and manipulating, denying it if anyone calls them on it, and making great excuses. Believe me—I know. I used to amaze myself sometimes at the stuff I would come up with when people would confront me.

Karen Yeah, and if your parents drink, you can always have some of their alcohol without having to buy any yourself. If they don't, you can always go to a friend's house or party. And if you seem drunk or you know others will be able to smell it on you, you can just hide, lock yourself in your room and sleep it off, or drink some coffee.

Eric Or you could use cologne or hair spray that smells like alcohol. Also, you could use mouthwash, gum, or mints to hide the smell on your breath. Some teens bring alcohol to school in water or juice or soda bottles—looks innocent, so no one suspects. If people do sense you're not well and ask what's wrong, you lie that you're sick to excuse a hangover. If you fall behind on extracurricular activities or schoolwork, you just say, "The coach or teacher hates me." It's hard to tell if someone is drinking, if they want to hide it and you're not looking hard enough.

Heading for a Dead End *Warning Signs That You or Someone You Love Is Drinking or Has a Problem*

Emile You have to pay attention to any changes in just about everything a person does—a person's attitude, habits, or appearance—that can't be explained. It can mean the person is drinking or has a problem.

Eric Like if any of your friends carry around lots of bottles or cans and don't want to share, if you find alcohol hidden in their rooms or other places in the house, if they use lots of over-the-counter meds for headaches or flu symptoms, or they use eyedrops, mints, mouthwash, or dark glasses to cover the effects, if they're stumbling, tripping, or looking confused or out of it.

Warning Signs a Friend Is Using or Abusing Alcohol

> Having friends who drink

> Being careless about personal appearance

> Having red or glassy eyes

> Stumbling or fumbling, not being able to stand up straight or walk

> Being lightheaded, having slurred speech

> Being tired, making repeated health complaints

> Having a family history of alcoholism or drug use

> Having diminished interest in hobbies or favorite activities

> Having mood swings, being irritable, overreacting, or withdrawing and isolating

> Avoiding loved ones or friends

> Having trouble paying attention or remembering things

> Having changes in school performance, tardiness, absenteeism, or disciplinary problems

> Experiencing changes in eating and sleeping patterns

> Acting irresponsibly or irrationally, being aggressive, starting arguments, breaking rules, displaying disorderly conduct, or having trouble with the law

> Feeling low, sad, or depressed

> Using poor judgment and engaging in risky behavior

> Lying

> Missing money, personal belongings, or alcohol around the house[16]

Obviously, losing interest in all the fun stuff you used to do together and making up lame excuses to avoid you, hanging out more and more with people who drink, acting out and getting into trouble, failing in school or missing extracurricular activities are all giveaways. Also, if they are abusive to others, careless about dress and cleanliness—like not showering, combing their hair, wearing dirty clothes, stuff like that—bells should definitely be going off.

Emile And then, if any of your friends have strange medical problems all the time, look depressed or sad a lot, and often don't make a lot of sense when they talk, you should worry. They might have just started to experiment with alcohol, or it could mean they might have been drinking for a while, and it's started to take over their lives.

And according to some stuff they gave me at rehab, *you* might have a serious problem with alcohol if you have these experiences:

> ❯ Can't predict whether or not you will get drunk
> ❯ Can't go without drinking for more than a couple of days
> ❯ Feel like you need alcohol to get through the day
> ❯ Believe that in order to have fun you need to drink
> ❯ Turn to alcohol after a confrontation or argument, or to get rid of unpleasant feelings
> ❯ Drink more to get the same effect that you used to get with smaller amounts
> ❯ Drink alone
> ❯ Remember how last night began but not how it ended
> ❯ Take alcohol to school with you
> ❯ Make promises to yourself or others that you'll stop getting drunk, but can't keep them
> ❯ Often feel alone, scared, miserable, and depressed without alcohol
> ❯ Have tried to stop drinking but couldn't

Eric Other things also tell you that you're in way over your head. All the bad side effects are signs you're in trouble—like binging and having hangovers a lot, falling behind at school and with your other activities, flying off the handle easily, or having health problems you never had before.

Saying "No" When It Counts
Handling Situations Where Other Kids Are Drinking

Karen Okay, so say you decide not to drink. The tricky part is when you hang out with kids who do and all of a sudden, you're in situations where everybody's drinking and you feel pressured. How do you do the right thing and avoid everybody thinking you're a loser?

Emile Kids face that dilemma all the time. It isn't easy. You have to be prepared with how you'll say "no."

Ashley Yeah, that actually happened to me just last week. I went out with an older guy I really like who's so cool and really popular, so it was like a dream. Then, he takes me to his friend's house and all of a sudden, I was, like, surrounded by kids who were drinking. I wasn't sure I wanted to drink, and I felt so out of place. I went from, like, having a great time to feeling like a total outcast in minutes.

Karen Sure doesn't sound like much fun, Ash. I feel for you. But Eric's right—if you choose not to drink, you have to be ready for situations like that. And don't feel bad about not drinking. If you stood up for yourself and did the right thing, you should feel good about it.

Ryan I totally agree. Saying "no" is the right way to go. Easier said than done, though. So here's how you do it without looking stupid. The passive approach is you take a glass and excuse yourself—then flush it down the toilet or walk around with it all night without drinking it. Or you could make an excuse—say you're not feeling well or that you're allergic to alcohol.

Blaming others is a good one too—say you've been in trouble with the folks for drinking before and don't want to chance it. Or say you have a game the next day and can't afford to be hungover.

You can also do humor. Say you pass gas when you drink, or say, "Not now, can't you see I'm busy flirting and looking cute?" This really hot girl I was chatting up at a party once said that—I thought it was so clever, it made me like her even more.

Karen There's also sarcasm—say you plan to give this "living" thing another try, so you're laying off the booze. Or that you're trying to quit. My brother used that one all the time—he is hilarious. And believe me, back in high school, not drinking never stopped him from being invited to every party on the planet.

Handy tip
If peer pressure to drink gets to be too much to handle, leave the party or situation.

Emile Also remember: You don't have to stay there. If the pressure gets to be too much, it's time to make your exit. Just head for the bathroom and slip out when no one is looking. Or say you're past curfew and take off.

Eric Another thing that works is going with other people who don't drink so you can back each other up. Deciding on some kind of hand signal to let each other know you need them to jump in or that it's time to leave also helps.

Ryan If all else fails, just say it directly: "Drinking isn't my thing" or "Not me." Yeah, you won't be the life of the party. The tradeoff is you won't get hurt, forget what went on, or be sick the next day, either. Most important—you'll live to talk about it.

Karen The people who are really your friends will not rag on you for not drinking. And those that aren't—well, seems to me it shouldn't matter what they think. A good way to avoid having to deal with any of that is to hang out with people who don't drink. Or plan something fun with friends that doesn't involve alcohol—hang at the mall, play a volleyball game, go bowling or Rollerblading.

Ashley God, I never thought of it like that. This is all really good stuff. Thanks, you guys! It totally makes sense, and I can definitely use it.

Jessica Yeah, you guys might have a point. I think I'm gonna give some of this stuff a shot. Maybe it'll help me avoid the pressure to chug every time I hang with my friends. It does, like, get old sometimes.

Emile Good, 'cause you don't want to become another statistic. Sometimes, it's a fine line, and it's very easy to cross. Just don't want to see anything bad happen to you.

Ryan Problem is, just because you aren't drinking doesn't mean others won't. And often you might depend on other people or you might feel responsible for them—especially good friends and siblings. So, you can still end up right smack in the middle of it.

Paving the Way *Helping Friends Say "No"*

Emile Knowing who does kick it with the booze and who keeps it dry affects many decisions you're gonna face. Like who you hang with, whose parties you go to, how ready you are to handle the pressure to drink, and how you stay safe. Of course, it's also good to know if the people close to you are hitting the bottle, so you can step in and offer help. Friends are there to support and look out for each other.

Karen Well, I think one of the best ways to keep friends or younger brothers or sisters from drinking is to set a good example—to be a positive role model by not drinking yourself and not encouraging them to drink.

Ryan And to help you feel good about not drinking instead of feeling ashamed, you and your friends can join or start an organization like

SADD: Students Against Destructive Decisions (www.sadd.org). It was started to help teens say "no" to drinking and driving. But now it's a peer leadership group that works to prevent any bad situations, like underage drinking, doing drugs, teen violence, and even suicide. I'm a member. I've met so many cool people and made some good friends who are all about good times without booze.

Karen Sometimes, though, even if you set a good example, your friends or siblings have different ideas and end up drinking anyway. They might even get sucked into it without wanting to. You might get concerned about some friends who are experimenting with liquor. You see them drunk and acting stupid and embarrassing themselves, but you just don't know what to do. You hang out less and less, and before you know it, you aren't friends anymore. One day, you hear how one of them got caught drinking in the bathroom at school or passed out at a party and had to be taken to the emergency room. I've lost more friends that way...but what can you do?

Ryan Well, if you really care about the person, you shouldn't give up on him. First off, you gotta say something. It can be hard, though. I knew my brother was drinking and doing other stuff way before the accident, but I was scared to bring it up. Thought he would be pissed and that if I told someone, he would hate me. Now I wish I had.

Eric Remember that speaker we had last year? That recovering college kid? He said it helps to prepare and practice what you're gonna say. You make a list of the bad things that happened when the person was drinking. You start with a very caring attitude so he doesn't become defensive and blow you off. No judgments or accusations. Try to find out how and why the person is drinking and how much. Then tell him you are there for him. The goal is to get him to agree to either stop or reduce his drinking.

Emile At my rehab center, they had a great model for supporting each other. It's called the Share Your Concern model.[17]

Share Your Concern

I CARE You tell the person you care and that you are concerned, how much his friendship means to you, and how important he is in your life.

I SEE You explain to him exactly what you saw him do that made you worry. (For example, you could say, "Last night at the party, you had five shots in less than an hour, and you started acting out of control.")

I FEEL You tell him how it makes you feel when he acts like that. (For example, you could say, "I'm worried because I've known you since first grade, and that isn't you.")

LISTEN You give him the chance to say what's on his mind or ask questions. This is the time to really listen and show him you care about whatever he says. No matter how upset or angry he becomes, you need to remain calm, stay focused, and avoid judging.

I WANT You tell him what you want to see happen. (For example, you could say, "I want you to talk to someone about how you've been acting when you drink.")

I WILL You tell him how you will support him and what you're willing to do to help. Again, you continue to tell him how much you care. (For example, you could say, "I really care about you, and I will help you find someone who can help you. I will go to the guidance counselor with you. You are my friend, and I am here for you.")

Ryan If it doesn't work, don't just drop it. You need to keep at it, so you can help your friends however you can, even if they hate you at first. Trust me, it could save their lives.

Emile Sometimes, tough love is the only way. Keep being there and bringing it up, and leave the door open for more talks, but if it doesn't help, go one step further. Intervene and get others involved—preferably adults you can trust. And be careful not to let yourself get sucked into drinking while you're trying to be a good friend.

What to Do If Someone You Care about Drinks or Has a Drinking Problem
❯ Bring up the subject in a relaxed and nonthreatening way.
❯ Find out why your friend, sibling, or loved one is drinking.
❯ Find out how much and how often he drinks.
❯ Find out where he gets the alcohol.
❯ Be a positive role model to let your friend know it is okay not to drink.
❯ Talk about it often—once is not enough.
❯ Tell your friend you are concerned and explain the problems and dangers of underage drinking.
❯ If you suspect he has a drinking problem, insist he gets help.
❯ Reassure him you care about his well-being and you don't think badly of him.
❯ Support and encourage him in his efforts to get help.
❯ Suggest a hotline, resource, or place he can get help or someone he can talk to.
❯ Suggest he talk to a child or adolescent psychiatrist or other qualified mental health professional.
❯ If your friend or loved one continues to drink without getting help, tell an adult—a parent, friend, teacher, school counselor, or family doctor—so he can get help.

Coming to the Rescue *What to Do If Your Friend*
Has Alcohol Poisoning

Emile Another bad situation to keep an eye out for is when someone has been playing drinking games like funneling or "kegging" and gets alcohol poisoning. Knowing what to do in a situation like that can save a life. Alcohol poisoning is not hard to recognize. Someone has it if they have any of these conditions:

> Are passed out (meaning you can't wake them up)
> Are semi-conscious
> Are throwing up while sleeping
> Are breathing slowly and infrequently (less than nine breaths a minute)
> Have a pulse that is fifty beats a minute and keeps going down
> Have cold, pale, or bluish skin
> Don't respond to pain like punching or pricking them with a pin
> Seem to be having seizures

Eric Okay, according to the pamphlet they passed out in gym class a couple of weeks ago, if someone has alcohol poisoning, you're supposed to follow these rules:

> Never leave the person alone.
> Never put the person to bed to "sleep it off."
> Get medical help immediately.
> Know the recovery roll and perform it on a person who is lying on his back.
> **Step 1:** Raise his closest arm above his head. Prepare to roll him toward you.
> **Step 2:** Gently roll him toward you, making sure his head is protected.
> **Step 3:** As he lies on his stomach, tilt his head to the side to maintain an open airway. Place his hand under his cheek to help keep his head turned to the side so he can breathe.

Now, even if you put the person in the right position, they might still have complications or die. You need to watch them carefully and make sure they're breathing. The person might also have been injured in a fall, or combined alcohol with other drugs, so another issue you don't know about might make the situation even more serious. So, the person needs to get to a hospital as soon as possible.

Drunk Driving *Don't Play That Game*

Ryan Yeah, alcohol can hurt and kill you in many ways, fast or slow. But it only takes one drink to kill you in a car crash. So, don't ever drive after drinking. If you're drinking, find a friend who's dry to drop you off at home. Or call someone you can trust and ask him to come get you. Or ask to spend the night and go home the next day. Don't get into a car with anyone who has been drinking, no matter how sober that person might act or look to you. Don't expect someone under the influence to get you home safe and sound—that's not something you want to leave to chance.

Eric If someone else has hit the bottle and is heading for the car, try to talk her out of it or just take her keys. If a bunch of kids are drunk and pushing you to "not be such a wuss and go for a ride," don't fall for it.

Ryan You can be "cool" without risking your life. I've gone over things a thousand times in my head—all the things my brother could have said instead of getting into that car that night. If he had, I'd still have my big brother.

Karen Yeah, also, if you know this kind of thing goes on regularly at certain houses and kids are driving after drinking, just don't go. If you know the kids' parents have no idea, it might be good to tell an adult who can take the next step—talk to the other parents, to the school, or whatever.

Jessica Yeah, right! And have the whole school think I am a total loser that rats on other kids. It's hard enough to fit in without having, like, a reputation as a snob or a prude. Instant social suicide!

Karen No—think about this. If your parents or adults at school handle it with tact, chances are no one will ever know who told, and you get to have a clear conscience about doing the right thing. Imagine how bad you would feel if something did happen to one of those kids—the guilt of knowing you could have said something and didn't.

Finding a Lifeline
Getting Help for Yourself or Your Friend

Emile Well, the good news is, if you, a friend, or someone else you care about is having a problem with alcohol, help is available. More than a million Americans have gotten help and are living healthy lives, free of alcohol. I am one of them. Proud to say today I've been sober for seven months and eleven days. So, it's important to get help.

Jessica How? What do you do? I think my boyfriend might need to talk to somebody.

Emile It's good that you're thinking about it.

Learning more about drinking and its problems is the first step in getting help. The second is admitting to yourself and others that there is a problem. The third step is realizing you cannot fix it by yourself and that you need help.

There are several places you can turn. One is your parents. But a lot of kids don't want to talk to their parents—they're scared of how they will react or afraid to be a disappointment. You can also go to a school guidance counselor, teacher, family friend, family doctor, minister at church, or anyone you know cares.

Ryan The next thing is to distance yourself from people who drink and avoid places where there's alcohol. The last thing you need is more temptation. This is especially true after you get help and stop drinking, in order to stay off booze and avoid starting up again.

Where to Get Help

Emile You can find an anonymous hotline for a local drug and alcohol program or call your local Alcoholics Anonymous organization. Just look it up in the Yellow Pages.

Eric There's also a great Web site, TeenCentral.Net, just for older kids and teens, where you can write in your issues, have other kids your age give you feedback, and have adult counselors respond to your problem with helpful advice. The Web site was created by the 125-year-old children's charity KidsPeace. You can imagine these guys know a thing or two about kids and problems. Give it a shot.

Emile   There are also hundreds of other sites on the Internet you can check out.

Web Sites

Alcoholics Anonymous
www.aa.org
This Web site of the international alcohol recovery support organization provides valuable information about quitting, including locations where support meetings take place, to help you in your recovery if alcohol has the better of you.

Hazelden Foundation
www.hazelden.org
The Web site of the alcohol and drug treatment organization Hazelden includes valuable information on drinking, alcohol abuse, and the road to recovery, which you can share with your friends and peers.

KidsPeace
www.KidsPeace.org
The Web site of the 125-year-old children's charity contains information about problems and issues you might be facing that could drive you to drink.

TeenCentral.Net
www.TeenCentral.Net
This Web site is especially designed for teens and offers anonymous, free, clinically screened advice to help you deal with the problems you face every day, so you can avoid turning to alcohol for comfort.

National Institute on Alcohol Abuse and Alcoholism (NIAAA)
www.niaaa.nih.gov
This Web site includes a section to educate you and your friends
on the science behind drug use and abuse.

Phoenix House
www.drughelp.org
The Web site of this alcohol and drug treatment and recovery facility provides
information on alcoholism and how you can get help for a drinking problem.

**Substance Abuse and Mental Health Services Administration
(SAMHSA)**
www.samhsa.gov
This Web site has a ton of statistics about the abuse of alcohol
and information on places where you can get help.

National Council on Alcohol and Drug Dependence (NCADD)
www.ncadd.org
This Web site contains useful information about substance abuse
and the terrible consequences.

Additional Resources

Web Sites and Articles

TeensHealth, "Drugs and Alcohol"
www.kidshealth.org/teen/drug_alcohol

**Talking with Kids about Tough Issues,
"Talking with Kids About Alcohol and Drugs"**
www.talkingwithkids.org/alcohol.html

**Neuroscience for Kids, "Alcohol and the Brain"
by Eric H. Chudler, Ph.D.**
http://faculty.washington.edu/chudler/alco.html

PBS Kids GO!, It's My Life, "Alcohol: The Basics"
http://pbskids.org/itsmylife/body/alcohol/article2.html

Students Against Destructive Decisions (SADD)
www.sadd.org

Books

Teens Under the Influence: The Truth about Kids, Alcohol, and Other Drugs—How to Recognize the Problem and What to Do About It
by Katherine Ketcham and Nicholas A. Pace, M.D.

Alcohol 101: An Overview for Teens by Margaret O. Hyde and John F. Setaro, M.D.

When Someone You Love Abuses Alcohol or Drugs: A Guide for Kids
by James J. Crist, Ph.D.

What to Do When You're Sad & Lonely: A Guide for Kids by James J. Crist, Ph.D., Eric Braun, Catherine Broberg, and Michael Chesworth

Alcoholics Anonymous (4th edition) by Alcoholics Anonymous
World Services

Everywhere you turn, someone's puffing away on a lit cigarette. The images hit you from every direction. And the message? It's cool, sexy, and rewarding to smoke. No wonder almost 46 million Americans are smokers today! And smoking has spread like wildfire among America's kids. Every day, thousands of kids across the nation take up smoking. Kids look up to their favorite celebrities, movie stars, singers, and athletes, as well as people closer to home, like their coaches, neighbors, and even parents. They admire these adults, so they copy them. Plus, smoking is still considered a rite of passage in a lot of social cliques, and kids find themselves under a great deal of pressure to go along with the crowd to prove themselves.

And that's just cigarettes. Tobacco can also be smoked in other forms that are gaining popularity as well, and smokeless tobacco is another big danger kids face. With all the bells and whistles tobacco companies throw into their all-out advertising campaigns—which zero in on the teen population as their number-one target market—what's often left out of the equation is the many bad things tobacco heaps on its users. The trick is to be able to say "no" to tobacco and avoid being teased, put down, or shunned by your friends at the same time. There is a way to do both. And it is the difference between making a choice that will keep you healthy and a choice that in the years ahead will cost you a great deal more than a couple of party invitations, snotty remarks, whispers, or glances—maybe even your life.

—Julius L. Licata, Ph.D.
Director of TeenCentral.Net

Jessica

HUFFING AND PUFFING AND BLOWING THE HOUSE DOWN

How Smoking and Other Types of Tobacco Can Wreak Havoc and Turn Your Life Upside Down

Ryan   Eric   Karen   Emile   Ashley

Breathing Deeply and Taking in the Facts
Smoking and Other Tobacco Products

Karen I can't believe it. Some kid on the steps outside just asked me if he could bum a cigarette. Do I look like a smoker?

Emile Relax, Karen. Maybe he was looking for an icebreaker to chat you up or ask you out or something.

Karen Well, if that's the case, he sure picked the wrong one. I can't stand the smell of smoke, and I've never been into smokers, so he blew his chance.

Ryan Well, it's his loss, and I don't blame you. I'm the same way with girls who smoke. Instant turnoff.

Jessica So he smokes. What's the big deal? If he's good looking, it's worth it, Karen.

Ryan Now why am I not surprised, Jess? Considering you get down with the booze, I don't doubt you smoke too.

Jessica Hey, cut me some slack, Ry. It's not like I hang out in bathrooms, surrounded by a cloud of smoke. Jeez. Can't a girl speak her mind around here?

Ryan Sorry, Jess. Say what's on your mind.

Jessica Well, yes, I light up every now and then. You gotta, like, try things—isn't that what growing up is all about?

Eric Well, that's a loaded question. It depends on what you're trying and what you're learning. But one thing I can say is you're not the only one. Every single day, almost 4,400 kids between twelve and seventeen try their first cigarette.[1]

Ashley Every day? Wow—that's, like, three times the number of kids in our entire school!

Eric Yep, it is a lot. And that's just cigarettes, which is what we all think of when we hear the word *tobacco*. Tobacco is a plant whose leaves are prepared for smoking, for chewing, or as snuff, so it actually comes in several forms. Smoking cigarettes, or even cigars, is one way to use tobacco. Cigarettes and cigars are legal—at least for adults over eighteen—and an estimated 20.9 percent of adult Americans smoke. That's 45.1 million people puffing away.[3] But even without the statistics, we know that because we see smoking everywhere—at restaurants, outside stores and shopping centers, at people's houses, your own house maybe, on the beach, and even on the school steps. And cigarettes are always easy to spot when you walk into a grocery store, pharmacy, or minimart—up front and close to the cashier, since he has to card you to make sure you're over eighteen. There's no shortage of brands, styles, looks, and flavors.

Emile Yeah, there are all kinds. A lot of kids I know are into those flavored cigarettes from India called *bidis*—they're basically tobacco hand-rolled in a *tendu* or *temburni* leaf (plants from Asia) and tied with colorful strings on the ends. They're cheaper than regular cigarettes and you can get them in chocolate, cherry, and other flavors. I tried them a few times, and they really give you a buzz. Then, there are *kreteks* or *clove cigarettes,* which have tobacco, cloves, and flavors. Kreteks contain 60 to 70 percent tobacco and 30 to 40 percent ground cloves, clove

Tobacco
a plant whose leaves are prepared for smoking in cigarettes, pipes, or cigars, for chewing, or as snuff[2]

I've Got This Friend Who...

oil, and other additives. Some people think they're safe because they're made from so-called "natural" ingredients that are used in food.

Ryan Some kids also use these water pipes called *hookahs* to smoke. They heat and burn the tobacco inside a big pipe that has water inside it. The water cools off the smoke, and sometimes the hookah even uses ice water, so it feels more soothing to your lungs when you inhale it through a long hose. Kids like water pipes because they look cool and exotic, and you can mix the tobacco with all kinds of flavors. Not as many people smoke hookahs, though, because they're big and not easy to hide or carry around, unlike cigarettes and cigars.

Karen There are actually several stages of smoking. There's *social smoking, moderate smoking,* and *habitual (chain) smoking. Social smoking* is when a person smokes only in social situations—to go along with whatever the crowd is doing. *Moderate smoking* is when a person smokes almost every day. *Habitual (chain) smoking* is when the person smokes all the time.

Eric Chain smokers are those people you see go through a pack or more every day, seem to smoke like eating candy, and always seem to have a lit cigarette in their hand. They're the type no one ever remembers seeing without a cigarette. My dad was like that for a long time, before he quit last year. It's still kinda weird not seeing him with a cigarette.

Smokeless tobacco
cut-up, dried tobacco leaves that are chewed and their juices spit out

Emile Then there's *smokeless tobacco*—also called *chewing, chew, dip, snuff,* or *spit tobacco.* Smokeless tobacco is not burned and inhaled like tobacco in cigarettes, cigars, and pipes. Instead, it's cut-up, dried

Types of Tobacco Use	
Social smoking	Person does not smoke every day, can go days or even weeks without having or thinking about smoking, and only smokes when in social situations when others are smoking
Moderate smoking	Person smokes almost every day and lights up even outside of social situations
Habitual (chain) smoking	Person has a serious addiction and can't go more than a couple of hours without smoking, smokes half a pack or more every day, and always seems to be holding a lit cigarette
Chewing, dipping, spitting, snuffing	Person chews and sucks cut-up tobacco leaves between his gums and cheek, and spits out the juice that collects

tobacco leaves that people chew and spit. You take a small portion, put it between your gums and cheek, and suck on it. You don't swallow the juice; you have to get rid of it. So, every few minutes, you spit it out.

Eric Tobacco contains *nicotine,* which is a drug. When people smoke, nicotine rides on small particles of tar. *Tar* basically contains the poisonous chemicals found in cigarettes. It is the brown, tacky substance that is left behind on the end of the cigarette filter. It stains a smoker's teeth and fingers and also everything else it touches—including your lungs—with a brownish-yellow color.

Nicotine reaches the brain about eight seconds after cigarette smoke is inhaled and in about three to five minutes after tobacco is chewed. It affects the *nervous system*—the system of nerves and nerve centers throughout the body, including the brain, spinal cord, nerves, and nerve tissue. It can perk you up like coffee does, or it can calm you down, depending on your mood and how much of it you have in your system. The immediate effects are an increase in heart rate and blood pressure, faster breathing, and squeezing of your blood vessels. So, it usually gives you a rush of alertness and energy.

Tobacco is the most widely used drug in our country, even though most people don't think of it that way. Here are some facts about kids smoking and using tobacco products.

Kids and Tobacco: The Cold, Hard Statistics

Statistics for High School Students
- Nationwide, about 28 percent of students reported using some form of tobacco in the past 30 days.
- On average, more than 1 out of 5 students (23 percent) smoked cigarettes. Girls were as likely to smoke as boys. White students (25 percent) were more likely to smoke than black (11 percent), Hispanic/Latino (22 percent), or Asian (11 percent) students.
- About 8 percent of students reported using spit tobacco at least once in the past 30 days.
- About 14 percent of students had smoked cigars in the past 30 days. Boys (19 percent) were more likely to smoke cigars than girls (9 percent).

Statistics for Middle School Students
- About 12 percent of students reported using some form of tobacco at least once in the past month.
- Cigarettes (about 8 percent) were the most common type of tobacco used, followed by cigars (about 5 percent), spit tobacco (about 3 percent), pipes (about 3 percent), bidis (about 2 percent), and kreteks (about 2 percent).
- Boys (about 13 percent) were slightly more likely than girls (about 11 percent) to use some form of tobacco. Girls were slightly more likely to smoke cigarettes; boys were more likely to use other forms of tobacco.[4]

Smoke This *Why Kids Get into Smoking*

Karen What I don't get is why so many people take up smoking. How could anyone like inhaling smoke or having that smell all over them? I don't even like to be in the same room with someone who smokes. And smoking is really awful the first few times. The smoke burns your eyes, chokes you up, makes you cough...I just don't get what makes tobacco, and smoking in particular, so appealing to so many people. It just seems really stupid.

Ryan I agree.

Emile Quite a few things do make tobacco—and especially cigarettes—a big temptation. Let's face it, there's a great deal of pressure for kids and teens to fit in and be accepted. So if you're hanging out with kids who smoke, you're going to be offered a cigarette. It's kinda like an initiation, and the other kids are gonna tempt you to "prove you're one of them." If kids that are already your friends start smoking, it's even harder to turn them down because you have history and you don't want to be considered a "traitor" who thinks he's suddenly too good for them.

Jessica Well, the way I see it, you don't have to, like, sign up to become a chain smoker. I don't see that much harm in one or two cigarettes if you leave it at that.

Eric Yeah, that's how it all starts. You start up because other smokers keep bugging you, even hassling you, to try it. Even though the first few cigarettes are a pain, they can be a lot less painful than being made fun of or put down by people whose opinions and approval really matter to you. The desire to be accepted has you hooked long before cigarettes or other substances even get into the picture.

Ryan Yeah, so for lots of kids like you, Jess, having a couple of cigarettes can seem like a really small price to pay to keep the friends you already have or make new ones. Me, personally, I don't buy into it.

Jessica But it's, like, something a lot of really cool, good-looking, famous, and admired people do. Like movie stars, singers, politicians. Everybody wants to look cool and in control. You can't help but be seduced by that. Am I alone here?

Ashley Well, no, I have to admit, if I see a guy light up, it does make him look, like, more grown up and in control.

Ryan Guys, you're just feeding into the hype. You see it as cool because you've been programmed that way by all the advertising and promotion

Huffing and Ruffing...

cigarette companies put out there. They're trying to sell a product that's actually bad for you.

Emile I remember exactly when I smoked my first cigarette. I was eleven, and I was hanging out with kids on my block who were a few years older. I really didn't like the taste, but I liked the respect—being "one of the guys." I was doing what the cool kids did and sticking it to my stepfather without him even knowing. Soon, I was inhaling, and at thirteen, I was a smoker. I guess what I'm saying is you might turn to smoking to rebel, to spite somebody, or show your independence.

Jessica I didn't even try a cigarette until I was sixteen. Now, I might have one every once in a while if other kids are smoking, but it's a social thing. And the water pipes—they look all exotic and make you feel like you're some character in a faraway land, like Aladdin or something, so I kinda get the charm. As for chewing tobacco—I think it's totally disgusting. I don't get it at all.

Eric Some kids go for water pipes or chewing tobacco because they think they're safer than smoking. And some people actually switch to chew to try to *quit* smoking. With chew, the whole looking up to celebrities is also a major motivator. It's big with baseball players because they can use it while they're playing.

Karen Then there are the kids who are really sick of the image they have—you know, other people seeing them as a "good girl" or "mama's boy." So they smoke as a way to get rid of that image and be more liked, get more attention, and be more popular.

Jessica Well, here's another reason. Both my parents smoke, and a lot of their friends do too, so I grew up around smoking. To me, it was, like, something grown-ups did. They don't want me to smoke, but how tough can they be on me when they started smoking at my age and still smoke every day?

Eric Oh, so if your parents smoke, then it's okay for you to smoke?

Jessica No, I'm just saying they'll be hypocrites if they lay into me about smoking.

Ryan There are also other reasons. Like, some kids get really nervous in social situations, and smoking keeps their hands busy, so they don't look as awkward and out of place. Or if they're just sitting around and are bored out of their minds, they might start playing with cigarettes to make things more interesting.

Why Do Kids Start Smoking or Using Other Forms of Tobacco?

❯ Because they're pressured by other people

❯ To show solidarity with a group and "fit in"

❯ To appear "cool" or even sexy

❯ To look more mature, grown up, or in control of their own life and destiny

❯ To look knowledgeable and worldly to other kids by knowing a new, exotic form of smoking

❯ To look tough or macho, like "a real man"

❯ To emulate and be more like their favorite celebrities or people they look up to

❯ To create a new image that makes them more liked and popular

❯ To "act out" and defy parents or get back at them

❯ To rebel against authority or society's rules and prove no one can tell them what to do

❯ As a rite of passage to adulthood

❯ To alleviate nervousness or the discomfort of social situations

❯ To alleviate boredom

❯ To have something to do with their hands, keep themselves busy

❯ To get a boost of alertness and energy[5]

Eric So, that's a whole bunch of reasons why kids give tobacco a shot in the first place. Now, if your friends happen to smoke every time you're hanging out, you're going to be around it a lot. Once you try it, there's no going back. It's not like you can just rewind and not smoke the next time they hand you one.

Ryan Same with smokeless tobacco—or whatever your poison is. Once you start, it's hard to reverse the process.

Emile That's how people go from being social users to moderate users to habitual users. They don't think much of it at first—they just do it because it's the thing to do. Before long, they start getting *addicted:* mentally or physically dependent, or both. And at that point, it's pretty obvious why they do it. Because they need to—because they can't stop. And soon they do it without even thinking about it, like a reflex.

Addicted
mentally and/or physically dependent on a substance

Ryan My mom, who's a psychologist, says there's another reason too. She says people never really outgrow childhood in some ways

❯ Tobacco heightens their senses at first and makes them feel more alert.

❯ As nicotine builds up in their systems, it relaxes them and makes them feel good, or calms them when they're upset.

❯ They're physically and mentally dependent on the habit and also on the way it makes them feel.

❯ They equate smoking with pleasure, fun, and even freedom.

❯ They crave a reward, and smoking gives it to them instantly.

❯ Smoking helps them satisfy a basic need for comfort.

❯ Smoking fills the need for companionship and security, keeping them busy when they have to wait for something.

❯ Smoking has become an automatic reflex, and they don't even think about it.[6]

and always look for ways to get back to that carefree, easy time, so a cigarette break is a chance to dodge responsibilities and "live for the moment." They get used to it, and going outside and having a cigarette is something they look forward to as a good excuse to stop working or studying for a few minutes.

Also, after working hard or accomplishing a certain task, they can reward themselves for a great job. My mom says having a cigarette fills their need for appreciation without waiting for someone else to recognize them.

Not to get all "shrink" on you guys, but my mom also says smoking satisfies basic cravings that are like eating and sleeping. A cigarette is always there, and by lighting up, the smoker feels less lonely. Smoking when you wait for something or someone makes the time pass by more quickly.

Eric Bottom line: There are more than enough reasons why people smoke, and most of them are not very good ones, but they really seem like good ones at the time.

Where Do They Get It? *Getting Your Paws on Tobacco*

Ashley Maybe I'm stupid or something, but I always wonder how kids, like, get cigarettes. You can't just buy them—you need an ID to prove you're old enough, don't you?

Emile Getting tobacco is the easiest thing in the world. A fake ID is real easy to get, and then it's a breeze. And you can always ask

Myths and Misconceptions about Tobacco

> Cigarettes and chew are legal, so it's okay to use them.

> A couple of cigarettes every now and then is no big deal and can't harm me.

> My parents smoke/chew, so it must not be that dangerous.

> My friends won't like me anymore if I don't smoke/chew.

> If I want to be part of the in-crowd, I have to do everything they do.

> I look so much cooler when I light up.

> All the cool kids smoke/chew.

> Using a water pipe isn't as harmful as smoking cigarettes.

> Chewing tobacco is not as harmful as smoking.

> I won't get hooked if I only do it once in a while.

> I smoke/chew because I *want* to, not because I *need* to.

> I'm not addicted to cigarettes/chewing tobacco unless I can't go a single day without them/it.

> I can quit anytime I want.

someone older to buy them for you. But you don't even need to go that far. In plenty of stores, they'll turn a blind eye because they want the money. I never had a fake ID, and I never got any grief getting hooked up. In the beginning, I got cigarettes from my friends, who got them from older siblings. Even some parents have no problems giving their kids smokes. I guess they figure it's better than their kids stealing them.

Of course, there are dealers who will get you cigarettes, but they make their real money selling drugs. They'll sell you cigarettes—at a really high price—but at the same time, they're trying to push drugs on you.

Jessica Since both of my parents smoke and my mom's a heavy smoker, there are usually several cartons at home all the time. I can take a few cigarettes or even, like, a whole pack every now and then, and my parents don't even notice. Also, my friend Katie's older brother works at this convenience store. When he's alone, he sells cigarettes to his sister and her friends. No one ever gets caught.

Ryan There are always ways to get around the rules with chew too. Some adults think it isn't dangerous, and they allow their kids to have it. And there are very few legal or even social consequences if you're caught using tobacco underage. As long as plenty of adults ignore the laws, kids will have easy access.

Exploiting Vulnerabilities
Tobacco Companies' Breadcrumbs to Chain Smoking

Karen So, what's the story? When are people most likely to start smoking? I've heard a lot of people say that if you don't start by college, you probably never will.

Ryan Sure seems like it. I read that nine out of ten tobacco users start smoking before they are eighteen.[7] And it's no wonder. Teens are the main target of the tobacco industry. We're the group that's most likely to start smoking and buy their products because we are desperately looking for acceptance and are easy to influence. Peer pressure is really hard to resist. Tobacco companies know that. That's why teens are their favorite target. The companies are required to spend millions of dollars to make sure the public knows about the tobacco dangers. But they spend *billions* marketing their product to young people, who are likely to provide the most new customers. And it's a domino effect, because teen smokers introduce lots of other teens to their first cigarettes too.

Eric Yeah, and they also know teens are more rash and less levelheaded when it comes to thinking through the dangers and consequences.

Ryan Tobacco companies work very hard to make tobacco look as cool and fun as possible to our age group, and they're succeeding. The first smoking experience for teens often leads to more smoking or use of other tobacco products. Lots of teen smokers become regular smokers well into their adult years.

Pretty Poison *Repercussions of Smoking and Other Types of Tobacco Use*

Karen Well, lots of information is out there about why smoking and smokeless tobacco are bad for us. And everyone knows it's illegal for kids.

Ryan One thing you already mentioned, Karen: Tobacco stinks. It stinks up your clothes, your hair, your room, your car, all your stuff, and your breath. And I don't know about you guys, but for me, that's like instant turnoff. My girlfriend has a cigarette every now and then with her friends, and when she's been smoking, I just don't want to be around her.

Karen   And speaking of instant turnoff, how about yellow teeth, brittle hair, chipping nails, bad skin, and early aging?

Eric   And the money it costs to smoke nowadays is ridiculous. Do the math. A pack of cigarettes costs about $4. If you buy just one pack a week, you'll spend $208 a year. And that's if you're still just a social smoker. Some people smoke a pack a day, which adds up to $1,460 a year! If you start when you're fourteen, by the time you're out of college, you will have wasted almost $15,000! You've just wasted the money for a new car, one year of your college education, or a down payment on a house.

Ryan   Then there's addiction. I mean, all smokers have probably said to themselves the first few times they tried a cigarette, "I'll never become addicted." I guess no one *plans* to become a regular smoker when they grow up. But "now and then" can become "all the time." Studies have found that nicotine can be as addictive as cocaine or heroin. People just don't realize how quickly addiction can happen. Then you're hooked, and there's no turning back. When people start smoking at an earlier age, they're more likely to develop long-term nicotine addiction than people who start later in life. Many kids start using tobacco by age eleven and are addicted by age fourteen. Six out of ten kids will still be smoking seven to nine years later.[8]

Karen   It's kinda scary when you look at the statistics. Every day, two thousand kids become regular smokers.[9]

Eric   Most addictions are both physical and psychological. The mental addiction is just as strong as the physical hold. And the cravings are immense.

Jessica   I see how much my parents smoke, and I have no intention of becoming like that. You just have to make up your mind and stick to it. I'm real careful.

Ryan   Well, it's great that you're so determined not to become a statistic, but I'm not sure it's that easy. And besides, if you don't want to be a smoker, then why smoke at all? Remember, even in small doses nicotine can be very addictive.

Emile   Now, you might say, "I like my cigarettes and I can't go without them. So, what's the big deal if I'm addicted?" First off, being a slave to anything in your life is no way to live. It means no matter where you are or what you're doing, you have to make time to tend to this habit—this monster.

Eric   Another reason addiction is bad is because of how dangerous tobacco is to your body every time you take it in and over time. Kids don't take it seriously because a lot of the dangers of tobacco might take ten or twenty years to develop. But time goes by quickly.

Tobacco contains hundreds of poisonous chemicals. You hurt your lungs and heart every time you use it. The main chemicals are *nicotine* (insecticide), *toluene* (industrial solvent), *ammonia* (toilet cleaner), *butane* (lighter fluid), *arsenic* (poison), *methanol* (rocket fuel), and *carbon dioxide* (fire extinguisher contents). So, you're putting stuff in your body you wouldn't even put in your gas tank. Nicotine, aside from being really addictive, is also extremely poisonous. It causes several types of cancer that are likely to kill you in time.

Let me put it to you another way: 400,000 people die every year from smoking! And 1,200 people die each day! Lung cancer is the leading cause of cancer deaths for both men and women, and 90 percent of all lung cancer cases are because of tobacco. Also, one person dies every hour from mouth cancer caused by tobacco. People who chew are 50 percent more likely to develop it. And if it's not cancer, then it can be chronic bronchitis, *emphysema* (a chronic, irreversible disease that destroys the tissue of the lungs), asthma, or heart disease. All courtesy of tobacco. Of the 4,400 kids and teens ages twelve to seventeen who try their first cigarettes every day, about half will eventually die from a smoking-related disease. That's more than five million kids who are alive today.[10]

Not to mention cigarettes cause one out of four fires. Almost every day, someone dies from a fire started by a cigarette.

Ryan   And if you don't die, at the very least, it can make it more difficult for blood to move around in the body, so you will feel tired and cranky a lot, and you won't be as energetic as other people. Because the smoke goes into their lungs, smokers often cough a lot and feel pain or burning in their throat and lungs. It definitely affects your lungs' development when you're a kid, because you're still growing, so you might run out of breath and steam more quickly than kids who don't smoke, which means less endurance when you're running or playing sports. So, for all the athletes, let's just say you won't exactly be at the top of your game.[11]

Emile   And that's just with regular cigarettes. Then there are bidis. Even though bidis have less tobacco, they have higher levels of nicotine, other harmful substances, and carbon monoxide. Also, because they're thinner, you need three times as many puffs, so you're getting more smoke in your lungs. They're also unfiltered. *Filtered* means having this spongy material at the end through which some of the tars can be held back from going into your lungs. It's the yellow part behind the white part of the cigarette that goes into your mouth. It traps a lot of the poisons, so

Filtered

cigarettes with a yellow spongy material that prevents some tars and poisons from being inhaled

I've Got This Friend Who...

you don't inhale them. Most cigarettes are filtered. But not bidis. That puts the smoker at an even higher risk for a heart attack, chronic bronchitis, and cancer.[12]

Smoking kreteks (clove cigarettes) is very similar. Some people think they're safe because they're made from natural ingredients that are used in food. But remember: Tobacco is natural too, and that doesn't make it safe. Cloves deliver more nicotine, carbon monoxide, and tar than regular cigarettes. So, they have a greater risk of causing lung damage, asthma, and other lung diseases—up to twenty times greater than the risk for nonsmokers.[13]

Ryan And hookahs? Well, they're marketed as being a safe alternative to cigarettes. This isn't true. The water does not filter out most of the

The Ugly Truth about Tobacco: The Danger and the Damage
Tobacco users typically experience these things:
❯ A high risk of becoming addicted to nicotine
❯ Increased stress when they cannot have a cigarette or chew
❯ Much greater difficulty quitting because of addiction
❯ Discoloration of the skin, teeth, and fingers
❯ Smelling like smoke all the time—including clothes, hair, and property
❯ Brittle nails and hair, skin damage, runny nose, and irritated eyes
❯ Decreased physical performance
❯ Greater risk of permanent damage to eyes, throat, bones, joints, and skin
❯ Much higher risk of sores inside the mouth or gum disease
❯ Higher risk for irritation of breathing passages
❯ Greater likelihood of developing bronchitis, chronic coughs, and asthma attacks
❯ Significantly higher risk of poor blood circulation, chronic lung disease, heart disease, heart attack, or stroke[14]
❯ Significantly higher risk of lung cancer
❯ Significantly higher risk of cancers of the mouth, esophagus, and pharynx
❯ Significantly higher risk of cancer of the head and neck
❯ Risk of stomach upset and ulcers when juice from chew tobacco is swallowed accidentally

tars. In fact, hookah smoke has concentrations of toxins—such as carbon monoxide, nicotine, and heavy metals—that are as high as or higher than those in cigarette smoke. Several types of cancer, including lung cancer, have been linked to hookah smoking. Plus, it has other risks that cigarette smoking doesn't, like infectious diseases—including tuberculosis and hepatitis—that can be spread when people share pipes.[15]

Eric As for chewing tobacco, the unusual flavors don't get rid of the dangers. Nicotine getting into your body in any form is unsafe and highly addictive. In addition to all the cancer-causing chemicals, chew also has *formaldehyde*—which is pretty much *embalming fluid* (a substance used to treat a corpse with preservatives to keep it from rotting)—and radioactive elements. Using chew to quit smoking is a big mistake because it actually has more nicotine than cigarettes. It can cause cancers of the mouth, *pharynx* (the cavity that connects the mouth and nasal passages with the esophagus), and *esophagus* (the muscular passage connecting the mouth with the stomach), as well as gum disease, heart disease, and stroke. Kids who use spit tobacco are more likely to become cigarette smokers too. And if someone accidentally swallows chewing tobacco, they can be really sick for hours.

Emile Smokers also put others at a much greater risk for health problems by exposing them to secondhand smoke. Plus, tobacco is called a "gateway substance" to alcohol and drugs. People get hooked, and they have to have more and more of it. At some point, maybe cigarettes aren't enough, so they look for something else. For some kids, cigarettes are only the first step because the same thinking that makes them try tobacco—whether it's peer pressure or the need to escape—can also pull them into alcohol or drugs. Check out some statistics I found:

What a Survey on Teen Smoking Showed
> Smoking is a major factor in potential drug abuse and depression among teens.[16]
> The association between smoking and having a drug abuse or dependence problem a year later is particularly strong.[17] Teen smokers were seven times more likely to use or abuse drugs than teens who did not smoke or use tobacco.
> Among tobacco smokers twelve to seventeen, two out of three have also used an illegal drug.[18]
> Among twelve- to seventeen-year-olds who smoke more than one pack a day, four-fifths have used an illegal drug.[19]
> Teens who remain tobacco free have a much lower risk of becoming involved with alcohol and/or drugs.[20]

Cigarette smokers are also more likely to get into fights, carry weapons, try suicide, have mental health problems like depression, or do risky things. So tobacco is a gateway to a lot of bad stuff.

Karen On top of that, every time you say "yes" and cave in when you're pressured, you miss an opportunity to learn to stand up for yourself. You become a "yes" man, and you don't learn to say "no" and draw the line when you aren't comfortable with something. If you don't learn to say "no" now, it will be a lot harder later in life.

Emile Also, there are *withdrawal symptoms* when you're trying to quit, including anxiety, stress, restlessness, shakiness, depression, head-aches, stomachaches, and feeling tired. Just like giving up alcohol. Who needs that?

Breath Mints, Incense, and Sock Drawers
Living with the Habit, Keeping It a Secret

Karen I know a lot of kids who smoke think no one will notice. They think if they play it cool, they can keep it a secret from people who might not approve.

Jessica It's actually easier than you might think. The smell is, like, obvi-ous, and it really hangs on hair and clothes. That's true. But it's easy to get away with smoking if other people smoke in your home, like my par-ents do.

Ashley Using breath mints to, like, get rid of the smell on your breath is the one I've heard most. I've also heard you stand outside and air out before going into the house.

Eric Yeah, and other people are always spraying air freshener or burn-ing candles or incense.

Karen My parents would have a fit if they caught me smoking. They don't smoke, and they both hate the smell, so they would notice right away. Don't get me wrong. I have no intention of smoking—ever.

Eric Well, the smell is really hard to hide. But a lot of parents just don't want to believe their kids are smoking, so they accept the excuses.

Emile Besides, there are other ways to hide your smoking. You can smoke out your window or in other people's houses. And as far as hiding

- Having cigarette smoke or tobacco smell in his room, bathroom, car, on his clothes, skin, or breath

- Hanging with a new group of friends who smoke

- Having discoloration on the fingers, stained or yellow teeth, blotchy skin, red eyes, runny nose, irritated throat, or mouth sores

- Having noticeable difficulty with breathing

- Losing steam or running out of breath often when doing sports or other physical activities

- Feeling unmotivated, tired, or irritable a lot

- Coughing or sneezing a lot

- Constantly using breath mints or eye drops, spraying air freshener, or burning incense

- Going to his room or bathroom a lot and locking the door

- Leaving windows open, even when it's really cold or hot outside

- Getting caught with empty or full packs of cigarettes, cigars, or containers of chewing tobacco

- Often making excuses for why he has cigarettes or other tobacco products on him

- Stepping out, "taking walks," or going over to a friend's house frequently

- Simply acting secretively, suspiciously, or sneaking around a lot

the stuff—like a pack of cigarettes, cigars, or chewing tobacco—nothing to it. There are many hiding places. And you can always ask a friend to hold cigarettes or chew for you.

Eric One major thing is the group you hang with. If you're smoking and you know the people you're currently hanging with won't like it, you drop them. Instead of having to face their disapproving glances or critical statements, you just cut your ties. A lot of people do that. Smoking just makes this rift between people. That's why most kids who smoke or chew only hang out with other kids who smoke or chew.

A Smoking Gun *Warning Signs and Symptoms*
of Smoking and the Use of Other Tobacco Products

Karen Well, I don't care what you say, Em. If you smoke or use other forms of tobacco, sooner or later, you're gonna get caught, especially if you do it all the time. First off, people will smell it in your car, in your room, in your bathroom, on your clothes, on your hair, and on your breath.

Ryan Yeah, and just hanging with people who smoke is a smoking gun.

Eric And your parents might start to wonder why you're always running outside for a few minutes. Or leaving windows open in your room when it's thirty degrees outside. Or buying air freshener and drenching your room in it.

Karen And if you're always running out of allowance or money you made working, and you have nothing to show for it? C'mon, who are you kidding? And spitting all the time if you use chew—well, that just speaks for itself. So does coughing like a maniac, clearing your throat a lot, or having red, swollen eyes from these so-called "allergies" you never had before that never seem to go away.

Emile Well, I know from experience that nothing drives suspicions quite like acting suspiciously. Always sneaking around, going for "walks," or locking your bedroom or bathroom and taking forever to open the door can't help but catch people's eye.

Eric Then, when you eventually get caught with cigarettes or chew—especially if it's more than once—bull's-eye! You know the saying: "You can fool some of the people some of the time, but you can't fool all of the people all of the time!"

Jessica So, what if you're concerned *you* might have gone too far and might have a problem with tobacco. How can you tell for sure?

Eric Well, as much as you might want to deny it and pretend there are no problems, there are plenty of signs. For one thing, worrying about whether you have a problem is already a sign. Another thing that should tip you off is if you seem to be lighting up all the time and making excuses. Stuff like, "I have this half a pack left, and it's a waste of money to just let it go," or "I need to buy a pack for that party coming up this weekend." Also, if you're constantly sneaking around, closing your bedroom door, stepping outside, or going over to friends' houses to have a cigarette, chances are you're past the social smoking stage.

Emile Also, having cigarettes with you wherever you are and always making it a point not to run out should be an eye-opener. Feeling agitated, moody, angry, or even sick when you don't smoke for a few hours are other signs.

Ryan Considering cigarettes or chew a reward and treat after working hard or doing well at school or at work and making time to take a break and treat yourself is a dead giveaway. If you aren't addicted, you

> Feeling really happy, satisfied, relaxed, and content when you finally light up or dip

> Always having smoking or chew on your mind and looking forward to the next time you'll have your next cigarette or dip

> Trying to quit and just not being able to

wouldn't treat yourself that way. You might go to a movie or have a piece of cake instead.

Eric Also, just take a look at yourself. Are your teeth yellow, your fingers discolored, your face blotchy, your eyes red, your hair and nails brittle, your nose always running, your throat always irritated, your mouth full of sores? If the answers are yes, you've been doing it for a while—a lot of it—and you wouldn't be unless there's a good reason—like being hooked.

Emile And if people associate you with cigarettes and think of you as a smoker, that's also a clue. Seeing yourself through others' eyes might help you see the truth about yourself.

Karen Yeah. And the mother of all signs is trying to quit and just not being able to because you feel like it's impossible to go without smoking for more than a few hours or days.

Getting over Being Tongue-Tied
Saying "No" and Helping Friends Do the Same

Jessica Well, face it, lots of kids smoke, even if it's only socially. So, if you have any social life at all, someone will offer you a puff.

Karen That's true. I used to be really good friends with this girl Julie. We had known each other almost since we were babies. Last fall, Julie invited me to a party at her friend Nicole's. Nicole's parents were away, and her two older brothers were actually the ones having the party. Kids were smoking and drinking. I didn't see any drugs, but I'm sure they were being passed around too. Julie just left me and ran off looking for Nicole. I got a juice, which kept people from hassling me about drinking, but I had to keep turning down one cigarette after another. It was ridiculous. Finally, Julie came back with Nicole, and they both had cigarettes. Nicole stuck one in my face and said "Here, smoke this." I said, "I don't think so," and didn't stick around long. Julie didn't even come after me. That was pretty much the end of our friendship. But the important thing is I said "no."

Eric Good for you, Karen! Way to stand your ground. Sooner or later, every kid is going to end up in a situation where other kids are using tobacco.

Jessica I remember exactly when I was offered my first cigarette. I met this guy, Chris, last summer. He's, like, a couple of years older and very popular. He invited me to hang out with him and some friends. We were cruising and all of a sudden, he pulls out a pack of cigarettes and lights up. Of course, he offers me one. I said "no" at first, but he, like, kept bugging me. He actually seemed annoyed. We were having a good time up until then, but the whole vibe changed over a cigarette. I finally gave in just to, like, break the tension. I didn't even inhale. I just let it burn out. But things went back to being fun again. It wasn't worth messing up a good time over one little cigarette.

Emile See, that's the kind of attitude that could get a person in trouble. Today, it's one little cigarette; tomorrow, it'll be something else much more serious. Drugs, crime—if you can't say "no" to a little cigarette, when are you gonna say "no"? Trust me—I know.

Ryan Yeah, Em totally has a point. You have to learn to stand up for yourself sooner or later. The way I look at it, you always have to put what is in your best interest first. No one else will do that for you. You have to keep in mind that it's not just about what's going on at the moment. A party is over in a few hours, but you have a lot of years ahead of you. Will I be more accepted by some kids at a party one night if I smoke or do whatever else? Probably. Will smoking or that other junk be good for me in the long run? Definitely not. Don't just live for the moment—consider your entire life.

Points to Remember When Facing Peer Pressure

❯ Standing up for what you believe and not letting others push you into doing something you don't want to do just for popularity or friendship is the way to go.

❯ True friends will respect your opinion—even if it's not what they think or believe—and will never push you into doing something that makes you uncomfortable.

❯ Learn as much as you can about people and places before you find yourself in the middle of sticky situations.

❯ When you start heading in the wrong direction, it can be difficult to turn back.

❯ If you don't draw the line on tobacco, you will most likely be pressured to try alcohol and then drugs.

❯ You will have to stand on your own and say "no" many times in your life, so the sooner you learn to do that, the more confident you will become in standing up for your beliefs.

Huffing and Puffing...

Eric And like we said before, a lot of kids think smoking will make them look more mature and independent. In reality, standing up for yourself and not letting other people brainwash you—having a mind of your own—is what maturity and independence are about. If someone keeps pushing you, hold your ground and don't let them get to you.

Handy tip

Prepare ways to react to peer pressure *before* you're offered tobacco.

Karen Second, you should pick your battles. Make it your business to know who does what, so you can make smart decisions about who to hang with and what to expect before you get into a situation you're not ready for and someone puts you on the spot. Then think about whether you really need to go to that kind of get-together. I'm very selective about the parties I go to after my experience with Julie.

Jessica If the situation does come up, how exactly do you, like, say "no" without rubbing people the wrong way?

Ryan Well, the way to handle it is very similar to the way to handle pressure to drink alcohol. You prepare beforehand how you're gonna react. You come up with some convincing excuses that can help you keep your cool but avoid caving in. Like, with me, I say, "It's just not my thing," when guys are dipping. But you could also say a whole bunch of other things.

Getting Past the Nagging:
Things You Can Say When Being Pressured to Smoke or Dip

"I have asthma, so I'm gonna pass on the cigarettes."

"I hate the way that stuff smells on my clothes."

"I have this toothache, so no, thanks."

"My parents are vicious—they sniff me like police dogs when I get home. There's no fooling them. They're former smokers, so they've done it all. They're one step ahead of me."

"You know, cigarettes and gymnastics don't mix. I'm gonna lose steam and run out of breath, and that's gonna put me behind. Not taking that chance."

"I have a meet tomorrow and my lungs have to be clean and clear. No hard feelings."

"No, thanks, I'm trying to quit."

"Gee, I would, but I'm kind of busy not smoking at the moment, and they don't really go together."

"My girlfriend gets real mad when I chew the stuff."

"I already got caught once, and my parents are watching me. If I get in trouble a second time, I'll get grounded for life. Would you guys rather not see me for the next two months?"

Bottom line: Where there's a will, there's a way. You can always find things to do or say to get yourself out of a tough spot without losing face or looking bad. There are plenty of options besides the straightforward and in your face "I don't smoke," but if nothing else, at least that shuts the person up and shows them you're not one to be pushed around. So, if you have the guts, go for it.

Cutting through the Smokescreen
Helping Yourself or Your Friend Get a Handle on Tobacco

Eric My dad smoked for over twenty years, and he had a really tough time giving it up. But he was determined to quit, and he did it. He hasn't smoked for almost a year now. But, remember, nicotine is highly addictive, and giving it up is extremely hard. After seeing what my dad went through, I would never want to put myself in that position.

Emile Yeah, I second that. Giving up cigarettes after you're hooked is hard. Took me a year to quit. It's real frustrating. I would go from hating that cigarettes had control over me like that to just not caring and giving in to the cravings. It's a struggle.

Ryan The bad news is no one can force you to quit or do it for you. You have to decide. You have to face that you have a problem and commit to giving it up. When people *do* admit to themselves they're smokers, they go through five stages.

Five Stages of Quitting Tobacco
The "Stages of Change Model" from the American Cancer Society[21]

Stage 1: **Pre-Contemplation**
> The tobacco user is not thinking seriously about quitting immediately.

Stage 2: **Contemplation**
> The tobacco user is actively thinking about quitting, but is not yet ready to make a serious attempt. The person may say, "Yes, I'm ready to quit, but the stress in my life is too much right now," or "I don't want to gain weight," or "I'm not sure I can do it."

Stage 3: **Preparation**
> The tobacco user intends to quit in the next month and often has tried to quit in the past twelve months. The user usually has a plan.

Stage 4: **Action**
> This is the first six months when the user is actively quitting.

Stage 5: Maintenance

This is the period of six months to five years after quitting when the ex-user is vulnerable to a relapse to smoking and must take steps and work hard to avoid it.

Eric I know from the information my dad brought home that there are programs out there just for teens who want to stop smoking. Some are a little expensive, but going it alone often doesn't work. You can also buy nicotine gum in the drugstore or get the nicotine patch—they're supposed to make it a little easier.

Karen So is making it a priority—and not putting it off. The sooner you think about quitting, make a solid plan, and work toward achieving the goal, the sooner you'll be rid of the habit. Give yourself a deadline—that way, you have a clear goal to work toward.

Ryan When it comes to giving up smoking, the most important thing is having a really strong desire to quit.

Emile Easier said than done. I never knew what a tight grip cigarettes had on me until I tried quitting. But people always say if you want something bad enough, you can make it happen. And reminding yourself of all the great reasons you're doing it and how it will make your life better is great help.

Karen Yeah, so is telling yourself all the time that you want to quit, and how much you hate it every time you smoke or dip. It helps you deal with the mental hold tobacco has over you.

Eric I know from my dad's experience that he still gets the urge to smoke sometimes, even though it's been almost a year. There are several things you can do. One is you have to separate yourself from people and situations that will tempt you, remind you of how it was before you quit, and pull you back in. If that means walking away from those "friends" you worked so hard to make—by doing things like smoking to impress them—so be it. It may not come to that, but if they hassle you, you gotta cut them loose.

Ryan Also, if you wanna put tobacco behind you, you have to change your habits and find healthy alternatives. If smoking puts you at ease because it gives you something to do with your hands, get rubber bands, key chains, puzzles, or crafts to keep busy. If it's the habit of having something in your mouth, munch on candy, sugarless gum, lollipops, raw vegetables, or sunflower seeds. Find other activities to entertain yourself so you don't turn to cigarettes from boredom. Things that give you a rush, a sense of achievement and pride, and are really great fun are the best things to pick—sports, clubs, volunteering, or a hobby or talent you're good at. And if you associate school breaks with tobacco, find something better to do, like getting juice, or talking to friends, or making plans for later.

Emile Here's something that works for me and for a lot of people. When the urge strikes, delay giving in. Tell yourself to wait at least ten minutes, then another ten, and another ten. Many times, that trick helps you get past the strong urge, and the next hour or day, you might crave it less.

How to Curb the Urge and Quit Using Tobacco Products

▶ Start thinking seriously about quitting. Expect that it will be tough and take it one day, or even one hour, at a time. Remember that you may be tempted to smoke or dip even years after quitting.

▶ Practice "mental affirmations." Continually tell yourself that you want to quit. Every time you light up or dip, tell yourself how much you hate smoking or dipping. This helps break the addiction's psychological side.

▶ Choose a plan that best fits your needs: a doctor's prescription for pills, a nicotine patch, nicotine gum, or a smoking cessation class.

▶ Set a time frame for quitting. Choose an upcoming quit date that will be significant so you can celebrate it monthly the first year, and then annually after that.

▶ Ask that your friends respect and support you in your efforts to quit. If they continue to pressure you to smoke or dip, change your social group. Avoid situations and people that tempt you to smoke.

▶ Change your habits by changing the behavior you connect to using tobacco, such as not smoking while driving or immediately after meals, or not dipping in the locker room before a game.

▶ Find activities to replace smoking or dipping and distract yourself from thinking about or needing to do it. Stock up on substitutes like gum, raw vegetables, lollipops, or rubber bands to keep your mouth and hands occupied.

▶ When the urge strikes, breathe deeply and picture your lungs filling with fresh air.

▶ Delay giving in to the urge. If you feel that you are about to light up or dip, tell yourself you need to wait.

▶ Review your reasons for quitting and remind yourself of all the benefits to your health, your finances, and your family.

▶ Stay committed to your goal to quit and work hard to resist temptation.

▶ Don't give up. If you break down and smoke or dip, try to quit again as soon as you can and continue to focus on the benefits of not using tobacco.

But also don't get depressed and give up if you do give in to the urge. It happens. Get back to your plan as soon as you can.

Karen Hey, do you remember that speaker we heard last year who was a former smoker and a lung cancer survivor? Remember he talked about deep breathing? Smokers breathe deeply when they inhale the smoke. So, he said, when the urge strikes, breathe deeply and picture your lungs filling with fresh, clean air instead.

Jessica What about helping friends kick the habit? I live with two smokers. You can go on and on about all the good reasons why they should, like, quit, but they'll always have a comeback. They know it will be really hard, and they're afraid to find out they can't do it.

Emile I know a little something about people getting on your case for smoking. I felt like I was being judged—like I was under attack. It would just stress me out, and then I needed to smoke even more.

Ryan That doesn't mean you shouldn't try to talk to friends. It's more about the *way* you talk to them. You have to understand, when people

Do's and Don'ts for Helping a Friend Give Up Tobacco	
Do's	**Don'ts**
▶ Be kind and understanding, working to earn your friend's trust. ▶ Let her know you consider her a good friend and you care. ▶ Talk about why you are concerned about her tobacco use and the dangers of tobacco. ▶ Offer your support whenever she wants to talk about quitting. ▶ Make it clear she can come to you when she is frustrated with her tobacco habit and/or has the urge to use tobacco. ▶ Let her know her previous attempts at giving up tobacco were good preparation for when she really does quit the habit for good. ▶ Offer to help her or get her help from others in any way she wants. ▶ Ask your friend how she is feeling. ▶ Make it clear you still love and respect her as a person. ▶ Find places to go with your friend while she is trying to quit that will reduce the temptation and help take her mind off tobacco.	▶ Don't preach, nag, or scold. ▶ Don't be judgmental about your friend's tobacco use. ▶ Don't put her down or ridicule her for using tobacco. ▶ Don't push her to decide quickly or demand that she stop using tobacco immediately. ▶ Don't focus on your friend's mistakes or criticize her for failed attempts at giving up tobacco. ▶ Don't approach a friend who is using tobacco as your "mission" or something you must "fix." ▶ Don't tell her it's easy to give up tobacco or show frustration with her if she's struggling. ▶ Don't refuse to talk to her if she doesn't stop using tobacco immediately.

are addicted to something, they totally panic at the thought of not having their fix. That's why smokers get upset when they're confronted.

Emile It usually helps to try to put yourself in their shoes. I don't mean you should start using tobacco, but you should think about how difficult their situation is and treat them like you would want to be treated. Being judgmental, preaching, nagging them, putting them down, or criticizing them if they've tried to quit before and failed won't do any good. Neither will treating them like a project or "lost souls" that it's your job to save. Friends who are in trouble need your understanding and support. Stay calm and remain positive. Tell them the facts about tobacco but don't push, and let them know they can always come to you when they're ready to talk more or need help.

Eric People who are trying to quit need a lot of support, so let your friends know you care. Once they know they can trust you, it will be easier to talk to you. You might also suggest to them at that point that getting the support of other friends and family members might be a big help too.

Where to Get Help

Eric There are a lot of places to look for more information or help and support with kicking the habit if you smoke or dip and can't seem to stop. The important thing to remember is that there's help out there and you don't have to just give up and live with this terrible habit that can kill you. There are a bunch of Web sites I know of that can be a great starting place.

Web Sites

TeenCentral.Net
www.TeenCentral.Net
This Web site from the national children's charity KidsPeace is a clinically screened teen Web site with a section about smoking that shows you how to identify whether you have a problem and how to quit.

TeensHealth
www.kidshealth.org/teen
This teen Web site from the Nemours Foundation teaches you about tobacco in addition to alcohol and other issues teens face.

Tobacco-Free QC's Youth Zone
www.tobaccofreeqc.com/youth
The Youth Zone Web site of Tobacco-Free QC offers you a lot of information on tobacco and quitting.

QuitSmokingSupport.com
www.quitsmokingsupport.com/teens.htm
and
GotToQuit.com
www.gottoquit.com
If you are serious about quitting, both of these Web sites help you to work through your tobacco addiction and kick the habit.

Campaign for Tobacco-Free Kids
www.tobaccofreekids.org
This Web site provides more information about tobacco and why it's not a good idea to use it—including some sobering statistics.

National Cancer Institute Factsheet on Tobacco
www.cancer.gov/cancertopics/factsheet/tobacco
This Web site offers some information about all the bad side effects and consequences of smoking.

The American Lung Association's Teens Against Tobacco Use (T.A.T.U.)
www.lungwi.org/tobacco/tatu.cfm
This Web site can help you serve as a positive role model and mentor younger kids.

Additional Resources

Web Sites and Articles

Campaign for Tobacco-Free Kids, "Smoking's Immediate Effects on the Body" (2004)
http://tobaccofreekids.org/research/factsheets/pdf/0264.pdf

TeensHealth, "Smoking"
http://www.kidshealth.org/teen/drug_alcohol/tobacco/smoking.html

Keep Kids from Smoking.com, "The Risks"
www.keepkidsfromsmoking.com/talkingtips_other.asp?src=overture

American Cancer Society, "Child and Teen Tobacco Use" (2005)
www.cancer.org/docroot/ped/content/ped_10_2x_child_and_teen_tobacco_use.asp?

Life's full of choices. Some are good and others are not. Why do kids turn to drugs? There are a number of reasons, and it's often more than one. Some kids are looking for acceptance, others might be forced into it, still others are curious, and others are desperate to escape from their problems. Also, when kids are depressed, moody, anxious, worried, or panicked, the body can react to drugs as if they are a solution. For a little while, drugs might make kids feel like they are no longer suffering from the pain or uncertainty that comes with such strong feelings. Drugs can also help them run from reality and feel popular, liked, energetic, capable, on top of things, invincible, and even like superheroes.

—Herbert Mandell, M.D.

There are various kinds of drugs—uppers, downers, opiates, hallucinogens, inhalants, and even legal prescription medications—and they come in many different forms—pills, powders, liquids, crystals, or plants and leaves. Each of them can be used in different ways, such as smoking, inhaling, snorting, injecting, or swallowing. The combinations are many, and the effects vary depending on the drug and the way it is used. They seem to be very easy to get, and their price has gone down significantly, making them that much more appealing. But taking drugs is a dangerous game with many bad and even fatal consequences.

—Nirmala Yarra Karna, M.D.

Once you get hooked on drugs, it is very difficult to have a normal life. Drugs change who you are in major ways. Your relationships with your loved ones can suffer dramatically, and everything else in your life can fall by the wayside. Drugs take the place of everything that used to matter and become the most powerful force in your life. There's nothing you wouldn't do—even things you never thought you were capable of—just to ensure your next fix. Your life turns upside down, you become a slave to the habit, and it can completely consume you. Breaking the spell can be very hard. If you do admit things are seriously wrong and try to get help, it is a process that requires time, your full commitment, and the strength to stick to being clean, which is a lifelong effort.

—Janet Sterba, L.P.C.

Emile

SMOKING, INJECTING, SNORTING...YOUR LIFE AWAY

The Quicksand of Drugs, the High Cost of Addiction

Jessica   Eric   Karen   Ryan   Ashley

The Twilight Zone Anatomy of Illegal Drugs and Mind-Altering Substances—on the Street and in Your Backyard

Ashley You guys are never gonna believe what I found near the tennis courts at school! A joint! And it had, like, already been smoked!

Jessica Yeah? So?

Ashley Well, isn't that weird? That someone would smoke it right out in the open and then just leave it there?

Jessica I know a lot of kids who smoke pot. So what? It's not that big of a deal.

Ryan Hear that, Ash? Drugs are way more common than you think.

Jessica You make it sound, like, so serious! It's just a little pot.

Drugs
chemicals or substances that change the way your mind and body work

Eric Well, the bottom line is it's still a drug. *Drugs* are chemicals or substances that change the way our bodies and our minds work. They might either intensify or dull your senses—like sight, hearing, touch, smell, and taste—make you more or less alert, and sometimes dull physical pain.

Legal drugs are not forbidden by law and are used for medical reasons to make you feel better or to heal an illness. But *illegal drugs* are against the law to have, use, or give to other people.

A joint happens to be an illegal drug in most places, except when it's allowed for medical reasons.[1]

Ashley So what illegal drugs are out there?

Emile Here are some types you may have heard of: heroin, X, coke, speed, Skittles, huff, G, Special K, roofies, and inhalants. Drugs come in all forms and shapes and can be used in different ways. Each involves different *drug paraphernalia*—any product, equipment, or material that is intended to help make, use, hide, or deal illegal drugs[2]—like pipes, straws for snorting, bongs, hookahs, or needles.

Eric Wow, how do you know so much about this stuff, Em?

Emile Well, it isn't something I'm proud of, but I'm no stranger to drugs.

Ryan Wait, I thought you had a problem with alcohol, Em?

Emile I did. My life was really tough for as long as I can remember, and home was hell. I needed something to get me through the day. Booze was my drug of choice. But in my "being bad" phase, I tried every other drug under the sun. And I was surrounded by people who used drugs as a way of life.

Yeah, it was one of the worst and stupidest things I've done in my life, but I did it, and a lot of other kids do it too, every day. The numbers I found will probably blow your mind. One of the biggest recent government studies on drugs found in 2001 that 28.5 percent of kids twelve to seventeen have tried drugs at some point in their lives. That's almost one of every three kids you know! And for people eighteen to twenty-five years old, it went up to 55.6 percent! So, more than half of the kids you know will try a drug before they turn twenty-five! On top of that, 10.8 percent of twelve- to seventeen-year-olds used a drug in the month before the survey was done, and 18.8 percent of eighteen- to twenty-five-year-olds did.[3] In the next hour, 15,006 teens will use drugs for the first time.[4]

Depressants
substances that slow the activity of your central nervous system and your bodily functions

Eric Okay, so let's talk about the most popular drugs out there. First, there are *depressants*—substances that slow down the central nervous system.

Emile The *joint* Ashley mentioned earlier is a nickname for *marijuana*. It is a depressant made from the cannabis plant. *Hashish* is another similar form of the plant.[5]

I bet a lot of kids you know have smoked a joint before, and you just don't know it. Practically everybody I know—both kids and adults—has at least tried marijuana.

Eric Well, some national reports say marijuana *is* still the most often-used illegal drug out there.[6] And these reports showed information from twenty-one major U.S. cities. Another survey done in 2005 found that 40.1 percent of the U.S. population who were twelve years old or older had tried marijuana at some point in their lives—97.5 million people![7]

Ryan Yeah, and the scary thing is, even kids younger than you, Ash, are trying it. According to this one huge study, 12 percent of eighth-graders,

Depressants (Downers)

Street Names	How It Looks	How It Is Used	What It Does
Marijuana			
B-40 Dope Ganja Grass Joint Pot Skunk Weed Wet	A green, brown, or gray mixture of dry, shredded leaves, stems, seeds, and flowers of the cannabis plant	▸ Rolled up in a small piece of paper, like a thin cigarette, and smoked ▸ Smoked in a pipe or bong ▸ Smoked in *blunts*—cigars that have been emptied of the tobacco and refilled with marijuana, sometimes in combination with other drugs ▸ Can also be eaten	▸ Intensifies your senses at first ▸ Later makes you calm, happy, and relaxed, like your worries don't matter and everything's fine ▸ You feel pleasant and see colors and hear sounds more strongly
Heroin			
Big H Horse Junk Skag Smack	Sometimes a white but usually a brown powder	▸ Most often injected ▸ Also smoked or snorted	▸ Gives you an intense feeling of pleasure followed by a sense of well-being and calm, and pretty soon, sleepiness ▸ You might also get *the nod*—a light sleeplike state where you're more sedated than actually asleep

25 percent of tenth-graders, and 32 percent of twelfth-graders have used or were using marijuana in 2006.[8]

Eric So, nobody seems to think marijuana is dangerous anymore. Well, let me assure you, it is. But it definitely isn't the only danger out there—that's for sure.

Jessica Okay. What else?

Emile *Heroin*—it's another depressant and also the most abused opiate, and a narcotic too. An *opiate* is a powerful drug that comes from the poppy plant and relieves pain. A *narcotic* is an addictive drug developed from opium that reduces pain and can change your mood and behavior.[9] Other opiates are *morphine* and *codeine*. They're used for medical reasons when a doctor prescribes them, and some pain medications are made from them, but they can be abused too and often are.

When I used to run the streets, I would see a lot of heroin going through people's hands. We could always tell when someone was using, especially if they were *shooting up,* because we'd see *track marks.* Or they would get "the nod."[10]

Heroin is serious stuff, but that hasn't stopped people from using it. Because it's extremely addictive, it's not as widespread, though. At some time in their lives, 2.4 million people will use heroin.[11] But only 1.5 percent of kids have tried it by the end of high school.[12] Even that's too many, if you ask me! You never know how pure it is when you get it, so a lot of people OD from it.

Ashley OD? What does that mean?

Emile If you *overdose,* or *OD,* you've taken more of a drug than your body can handle. You can OD on other drugs too. There's *cocaine* and *methamphetamine*. They're both *stimulants*—substances that make your heart beat faster. Just for comparison, so is coffee, but it's not illegal.

Jessica Cocaine is one that most people have heard of. I've actually seen people do cocaine. Isn't it sometimes called *nose candy*?

Emile Right, and also other names, including *crack*—cocaine that's especially processed for smoking.

Cocaine is widespread. In 2005, almost 14 percent of all people twelve years old and older had tried it at least once—that's 33.7 million Americans. And 8 percent of kids have tried it by the end of high school.[14]

Shooting up
taking heroin intravenously through a needle

Track marks
the telltale red and blue marks left up and down a heroin addict's arms that result from regular needle use

OD (overdose)
taking more of a chemical substance than your body can handle, which can make you seriously ill or even kill you

Stimulants
substances that cause your heart to beat faster, your blood pressure and body functions to increase, and make you feel more energetic[13]

Eric The National Institute on Drug Abuse (NIDA) reported in 2004 that *coke* was an epidemic in all twenty-one major cities studied in 2002, and it was responsible for more emergency room visits than any other drug in seventeen of those twenty-one cities. So it's everywhere!

Amphetamines are powerful stimulants that fuel you with energy. *Methamphetamine,* or *meth,* is the most powerful of them all. The smokable form is mostly known as *ice* or *crystal meth,* and people also call it *speed* because of its effects. You feel like you're running at the speed of light, and you aren't hungry or tired. You can get so much done and just keep going.[15]

Emile Yeah, and because of that first powerful rush, ice users keep chasing the high and want more and more. You figure you've found the secret formula to never losing steam and the ability to keep going when all other chemicals wear off.

Stimulants (Uppers)

Street Names	How It Looks	How It Is Used	What It Does
Cocaine			
Blow C Coke Crack Flake Nose candy Snow	Most often a white powder	› Most often cut into separate lines or strips on a flat, smooth surface (like a glass table, a glass tray, or a mirror) and snorted up a user's nose through some kind of straw › Also injected or smoked	› Makes you feel like you're on top of the world and have limitless power and energy, including the strength and capability to do anything
Methamphetamine			
Biker's coffee Chalk Crank Crystal meth Glass Ice Meth Speed Stove top Yellow bam	Comes in many different forms but is best known as tiny, clear crystals	› Used in many different ways, including snorted, swallowed, injected, or smoked	› When smoked or injected, gives you a really powerful rush that lasts a few minutes and makes you feel like you can move a mountain, followed by a feeling of calm, contentment, and relaxation › When swallowed or snorted, the high can last from eight to twenty-four hours and throws you into a state of hyperactivity

Eric Meth is becoming the next epidemic in this country. In many western and midwestern states, it's the most frequently used drug besides alcohol and marijuana.

Emile Another group of drugs—*hallucinogens*—are very strong drugs too. You know, Ecstasy, LSD, PCP, magic mushrooms.

Hallucinogens cause you to see things differently or experience things that aren't really there. You feel like you're in this dream state where all these really interesting and unbelievable things happen. The effects are pretty unpredictable, though, so you never know how they're gonna hit you. You could have a really good *trip*—the high or effect of the drug—or a really bad one, and you can't control how it turns out. And each time is different. A lot of it depends on the amount you take—it's never an exact science—and also what's around you and,

Hallucinogens

Street Names	How It Looks	How It Is Used	What It Does
Ecstasy (MDMA)			
Adam E Love drug Roll X XTC	A pill or some sort of powder	❯ Usually swallowed ❯ Also snorted	❯ Makes you hyperenergetic and sharpens your senses ❯ You feel like you can keep going for days without stopping ❯ At the same time, you hallucinate
PCP			
Angel dust Ozone Rocket fuel Wack	A white crystal-like powder, some sort of colored powder, or a pill	❯ Snorted ❯ Also smoked or swallowed	❯ Causes hearing and sight distortions ❯ Causes flashbacks to things that happened in the past or dreams you may have had before
LSD			
Acid	A pill or even some sort of liquid	❯ Usually swallowed	❯ Causes hearing and sight distortions ❯ Causes flashbacks to things that happened in the past or dreams you may have had before
Magic Mushrooms			
Shrooms	Actual hallucinogenic mushrooms	❯ Eaten ❯ Boiled in tea ❯ Eaten with food	❯ At low doses, effects can feel similar to smoking pot ❯ At high doses, produce hallucinations and a sense of euphoria

believe it or not, your personality and expectations. From what I've read, about 6.5 percent of kids have tried hallucinogens before they graduate from high school.[16]

Karen Well, I've definitely heard of Ecstasy. Who hasn't? That's E, right?

Eric Yep. *Ecstasy* is the most popular nickname of the drug *MDMA*. It's both a stimulant and a hallucinogen with all the effects of both. It's the designer drug that's really popular at raves and techno clubs. It gets your blood pumping, and its effects last about six hours. It's a relatively new drug and has become more popular only in the last ten years.[17]

Emile *PCP* is another hallucinogen. When it's combined with marijuana, people call it *killer joints* and *crystal supergrass.*

   LSD is yet another hallucinogenic drug. Its effects last twelve hours or more.[18]

   There are *magic mushrooms* too, also known as *shrooms*—actual mushrooms that have a powerful hallucinogenic effect that lasts about four to five hours.[19]

Eric The drugs we just talked about are all illegal drugs, so you have to get them secretly from dealers. But, you don't have to work that hard to get some of the same effects with chemicals that are completely legal and cheaper. It's much more tempting when kids don't need to make risky back-alley money swaps that can get them arrested or hurt.

Ashley Like what kinds of chemicals are you talking about?

Over-the-counter medicines, inhalants, prescription drugs
legal chemicals that when misused result in the user experiencing mind-altering effects

Ryan Well, I've heard of kids buying *over-the-counter cough and cold medicines* to get high. The main ingredient in many cough syrups, tablets, capsules, gel caps, and lozenges is *dextromethorphan,* or *DXM,* which has alcohol in it.

Eric Kids also pick up other over-the-counter substances called *inhalants,* like spray paint, hair spray, lighter fluids, correction fluid, cleaning fluids, paint, or glue from the local hardware store. When kids *huff* them—inhale, sniff, or snort them—they get a buzz.[20]

Ashley I've heard of huffing! I remember some kids at my last school talking about that.

Ryan A lot of kids are using inhalants for a high, because they're so easy to get and pretty cheap. In 2005, 16.1 percent of eighth-graders, 13.3 percent of tenth-graders, and 11.1 percent of twelfth-graders reported that they've done inhalants.[21]

Legal Substances with Drug-like Effects

Street Names		How It Looks	How It Is Used	What It Does
Over-the-Counter Drugs **cough and cold medications containing dextromethorphan (DXM)**				
Candy DM Orange Crush Red devils Robo	Skittles Triple C Tussin Velvet Vitamin D	Cough syrup, tablets, capsules, gel caps, lozenges, or a powder	› Swallowed › Sucked on › Snorted	› Cause the same effects as alcohol and other depressants › At first, your senses become more intense and your emotions become stronger › Later, you become calm, happy, blissful, and drowsy
Inhalants				

Air blast
 Bolt
 Boppers
 Bullet
 Buzz bomb
 Hippie crack
 Huff
 Laughing gas
 Moon gas
 Oz
	Pearls
	 Poor man's
	   pot
	 Satan's secret
	 Shoot the
	   breeze
	 Spray
	 Texas shoe
	   shine
		Spray paint, hair spray, lighter fluids, correction fluid, cleaning fluids, paint, or glue	› Inhaled or sniffed
			 › Snorted
				› Usually cause you to feel "drunk," slow down, and become disoriented, calm, happy, or carefree

Prescription Drugs **Fentanyl, OxyContin, Dexedrine, Demerol, Ritalin, Adderall, Seroquel, Xanax, Valium, Vicodin**				

Apache
 Bars
 Bennies
 Black
   beauties
 C
 Candy
 China girl
 China white
 Crosses
 Dance fever
 Demmie
 Downers
 Friend
 Goodfella
 Hearts
	Hillbilly
	   heroin
	 Hydro
	 Jackpot
	 Killer
	 O
	 Oxy
	 Oxycotton
	 Sleeping pills
	 Tango & Cash
	 TNT
	 Tranks
	 Truck drivers
	 Vikes
	 Xanies
	 Zs
		Pills, some type of liquid, or a powder	› Injected
			 › Snorted
			 › Swallowed
			 › Smoked
				› Have the characteristic effects of stimulants, depressants, or opiates, depending on the particular prescription drug

Eric To make matters worse, kids are getting their hands on *prescription drugs,* usually right out of their family medicine cabinets. They can be stimulants, depressants, or opiates. These come in a variety of forms.[22]

Some prescription drugs are prescribed by a doctor to help people with depression, calm them down, or put them to sleep when they're really stressed. They're called *barbiturates*—also known as *downers, barbs, red devils, blue devils,* and *yellows.*[23]

Ryan In 2005, 9.5 percent of twelfth-graders ranked the prescription drug *Vicodin* as the most commonly abused drug. The same survey showed that the abuse of *OxyContin* increased 40 percent among twelfth-graders from 2002 to 2005.[24]

Eric And the 2004 NIDA study found that the prescription drug *fentanyl,* which is a narcotic fifty to a hundred times stronger than morphine, is being combined with cocaine and heroin. They're calling it the "killer drug combination" because it's very dangerous and it's killed a bunch of people recently![25]

Pharming parties
parties at which kids bring and trade prescription drugs

Emile Have you guys heard of "pharming parties"? That's when kids swipe some of these prescription drugs and bring them to a party to swap with other kids who bring other prescription drugs. Each drug gets a specific rating, and the trading is based on that rating. Really dangerous!

Jessica My older cousin warned my friends and me about, like, *club drugs* or *date-rape drugs*. He said he was going to *raves* (all-night dance parties with techno music and strobe lights) in college. Some guys were using these drugs to, like, get girls alone and take advantage of them. The next day, the girls couldn't remember a thing that happened!

Club drugs or date-rape drugs
drugs dissolved in liquids so the person isn't aware of ingesting the drug and experiences memory loss

Ashley That is beyond scary! Almost makes me never want to go to a rave!

Ryan The thing is, these drugs are becoming much more mainstream these days. It doesn't just happen at raves anymore. You could just be at a house party or even a dance at school or a bonfire, and if you're not careful, somebody could slip you something. They just drop it in your glass, and it's lights out.

Emile I know of three of these drugs: *GHB, Rohypnol,* and *ketamine.*[26] GHB and Rohypnol affect you a lot like alcohol. So, if somebody drops one in your glass, no one will suspect anything's wrong. They'll just think you've had too much to drink.

Taking ketamine feels similar to drinking, but the effects happen very quickly. Most important, it makes you forget things too.

Street Names	How It Looks	How It Is Used	What It Does
GHB (gamma hydroxybutyric acid)			

G
Georgia
  homeboy
Grievous bodily
  harm
Liquid Ecstasy
	Usually an odorless, colorless liquid, but can also be a powder	› Generally swallowed	› Creates a pleasant, peaceful, and drowsy feeling

Rohypnol			
Forget-me pill Roche Roofies	Usually a pill, but can also be a powder	› Generally swallowed	› Creates a pleasant, peaceful, and drowsy feeling
Ketamine			
Cat Valium Special K Vitamin K	A liquid or a powder	› Generally swallowed	› Causes the absence of any pain, like an anesthetic › You fall into a mellow, colorful, dreamlike state with small doses, experiencing colors and sounds much more intensely › Large doses commonly lead to intense hallucinations and blackouts

Eric Yeah, I heard ketamine is a general anesthetic doctors and veterinarians use sometimes. It makes you hallucinate and then knocks you out completely—making you feel nothing.

Why Throw the Dice? *Gambling with Life*
When There's So Much to Lose

Karen So, why are so many kids giving drugs a shot and even using them on a regular basis? Seems to me like you'd only be asking for trouble.

Emile Well, we kids are curious about the world, and we're so eager to try anything. When somebody tells us something's worth taking and they sound like they know what they're talking about, we can't resist. If I had a buck for every time someone said to me, "It's really cool—just try it.

It's no big deal!" I'd be a rich guy. That's the thing. A lot of kids are trying to figure out what the "big deal" really is. You know, what does it feel like to smoke, use, snort, down pills, or shoot up? What's it like to get high? I think a lot of kids hear all this hype from their friends, and they just want to find out for themselves the answers to those questions. It's all about the novelty.

Ryan And peer pressure is a huge part of the problem too. Our friends, social groups, and boyfriends and girlfriends are all real important to us. Of course we feel pressure to fit in and do what the crowd is doing. If they're experimenting with drugs and pushing them on us, it's hard for us to draw the line and just pass. Especially if we believe the lie that "everyone is doing it," or we think it will help us look or act cooler, or change our image in some way that will make us more popular or liked. It's especially hard to say no if kids are minimizing the seriousness of the drug by saying, "It's only weed." You trust your friends and you rely on their word. Nobody thinks their friends would hurt them on purpose. Other kids think drugs make them seem more fun, outgoing, grown up, or independent. Or they believe drugs help people be more open and feel closer to each other, and sometimes kids want that closeness so much— maybe because they don't have it at home or they have few friends—that they're willing to do anything for it. They might think drugs give them an "in" with people they would never otherwise dare talk to.

Emile For kids who are in a gang or hanging with a "bad" crowd, peer pressure goes to a whole new level. It can be brutal! You're supposed to prove you're tough in every way, and using drugs is definitely one way. But the truth is, the pressure doesn't always come just from friends. It can come from your family life too. If there are problems at home, drugs can make you feel good or make your troubles seem far away. So, when everyday problems are getting the better of you, escaping even for a little bit is very tempting.

Eric Yeah, and on top of that, if family members are using drugs and doing them in front of you, of course that's gonna send you the message it's all good, and that can lead you to take the step yourself.

Ashley It's hard to imagine my parents influencing me to *try* drugs. They would totally wig if I ever did anything like that!

Jessica Mine, too, but get this: This one friend of mine once got caught, like, smoking pot, and believe it or not, his parents actually called it a "step on the road to adulthood" and just brushed it off. They told him to watch himself and not get carried away. Can you believe that?

Eric School problems can have an impact too. Some kids turn to drugs to help them cope, work harder, handle the pressure more calmly, take the edge off, or just plain leave their worries behind. Whatever you need—whether it's to keep going or to wind down and get some rest—drugs seem like that instant fix.

Ryan Yeah, adolescence is a time of major pressure overall. We have more to do at school, big expectations placed on us, new experiences, and social and sexuality issues too—big time. Teens could turn to drugs to comfort them and reduce that huge emotional turmoil. That's what I think happened to my brother—he had so much going on, he just couldn't handle it all. Somebody said "Hey, give this or that a shot," and he was so desperate he was ready to try anything.

Karen And let's face it: Some kids try drugs just because they think it'll be fun. They could be bored out of their minds and looking for thrills. Other times, kids are rebelling against other people's rules. They just want to make a statement and prove they'll do whatever they want, and no one can tell them anything or stop them from being their own boss.

Ryan Well, another reason is if they have a physical condition or some mental issue like depression, anxiety, a mood problem, or fears. Drugs

Why Do Kids and Teens Try Drugs?

> Experimentation—out of curiosity

> Peer pressure—their friends are pushing it on them and they want to be accepted

> Gang association or hanging out with the "wrong" crowd

> Desire to appear more cool or grown up

> Desire to develop closeness with other people based on a shared experience

> Family problems pushing them over the edge

> Family members setting an example

> School pressure being too much for them to take

> Boredom getting to them and making them seek out thrills

> Rebellion against social norms

> Need to "medicate" depression, anxiety, or fears, or just to feel better

Myths about Drugs
❯ Everyone is doing it.
❯ It's no big deal—it's just some harmless fun.
❯ It will make me more fun, outgoing, cool, mature, independent, or likable to others.
❯ Drugs help make people more open-minded and bring them closer together.
❯ If your friends are doing drugs and telling you it's okay, then it must not be that bad.
❯ If your parents are doing drugs, then it must be okay for you to do them too.
❯ Drugs will take your mind off your problems and make you feel better.
❯ Some drugs are not as bad as others.

"medicate" them and make these things less bothersome and more bearable. So, they might see drugs as helpful.

Eric Whatever the case, I think a lot of kids feed into the myths about drugs, and it makes it easier for them to get sucked into using them.

Ashley One thing I can't figure out is, how are kids getting the drugs?

Emile If you want drugs, it is so easy to get your hands on them. Drugs aren't just a thing you score in dark alleys any more. More and more, they're moving into mainstream society. The suppliers are everywhere—in schools, in office buildings, at health clubs, and even at malls. And the users can be anybody, from all walks of life—lawyers, teachers, coaches, engineers, librarians, housewives, you name it. So, of course, it's the same for kids from every walk of life too.

Ryan I guess the fact that they're so easy to get these days also makes them harder to resist.

Karen Well, don't people need a lot of money, especially when they're doing drugs on a regular basis?

Emile It's not as expensive as you might think to score some drugs. If kids are getting prescription drugs from the family medicine cabinet, they're obviously free. But getting them outside your house is affordable too. The drug culture drives this weird sense of sharing, where no one seems selfish at first. Everybody is pushing drugs into your hands. Once you become a part of the culture, it seems like everyone supports each other's habits. People are generous because a lot of them don't like to do drugs alone—unless they're addicts, in which case, they couldn't care less.

But if you do have to put up the cash for them, most drugs aren't that expensive anymore. If you have a part-time job, you can afford to keep buying. As you get sucked deeper and deeper, and you need larger and larger amounts, you might have to get a little creative—like borrowing money from people. Some kids steal from their parents' wallets or sell stuff to pay for it. Other kids might even break and enter or rob a store. But usually, it doesn't have to be that drastic. Just to give you an idea of the cost, one ounce of marijuana runs about $100 to $200, depending on what city you're in. Two grams of cocaine (enough for a couple of hits) are around $110, and two grams of heroin are about $120.[27]

First Roll of the Joint, First Roll of the Dice
The Age of Vulnerability

Ashley So why do some kids try drugs, while others manage to resist them?

Eric Well, a lot of times, a step up to drugs is cigarettes. Tobacco is a *gateway substance*—something that opens the door to trying alcohol and drugs. So, if you smoke, you're more likely to drink or do drugs, and once you try one drug, it's a domino effect. It's only a matter of time before you try others.

Karen Going into high school is another vulnerability that can expose kids to drugs. It's such a big deal because it's a major change in kids' lives. It's kind of an initiation—kids become teens, and there are so many new expectations, experiences, and opportunities. It can be overwhelming, and some kids become desperate for ways to make sense of it all. Drugs might become tempting because they seem to help in some ways, so junior high school kids and high school freshmen are particularly vulnerable to getting sucked into drugs because they're trying to find their place and make new friends.

Eric Also, the early teen years are a time when some mental problems like depression, bipolar disorder, and anxiety start to hit. If the feelings they bring on confuse and scare you, you might look to drugs as a "temporary fix" to make you feel better. Those problems also have physical symptoms that can be really unpleasant, and your body can react to drugs like they're a solution.

Karen It's not just teens who are so easily influenced. Believe it or not, younger kids are really vulnerable to social pressures. I read that peer pressure from classmates starts as early as preschool. Kids with low self-esteem, or who don't have a good, solid, caring family or who are missing a sense of belonging are particularly vulnerable to peer pressure. If somebody else offers them a chance to be part of something and share a bond that makes them "family," they're all too eager to jump in with both feet. But they're still too young and naïve to understand all the bad consequences of drugs. So, it's a risky time. And also, during puberty, kids still haven't figured out all the social stuff and the whole awkward thing around kids of the opposite sex, but they face those situations more. So, they're even *more* likely to turn to drugs to ease the nerves and discomfort.

Eric And also, if they think drugs are the "in" thing, they're tempted to try them so they can fit in with older kids.

Deadly Games *The High Price of Doing Drugs*

Emile Well, I can tell you from plenty of personal experience that drugs might seem cool at first, but all the bad consequences just aren't worth the high.

Eric There is a fine line between taking the recreational drug now and then and getting hooked. Drugs are a sure thing when it comes to changing how you feel—especially when you aren't feeling that great. They make you feel different—usually better in some way at first, if you do them in small doses. They also have a way of bringing you and other people together, creating the illusion you're all really close. So, if you try them once, you're walking the line. And if you have a good experience, the temptation to keep using just gets stronger. When you try one drug and it goes well, you get braver and more likely to try another...and another. The more you use, the more they take over your mind, body, and spirit. Plus, the high of the drugs you're already using gradually wears off, so you're always on the lookout for something new, hoping to get a better high. You become a guinea pig for every new batch of drugs to hit the streets.

Addiction
being mentally and/or physically enslaved to a habit, practice, or substance

Emile Plus, if you're hanging out with people who do drugs often, what are you going to do—try them once and then watch the rest of the time? Of course not. You'll end up going along. And little by little, that leads to *addiction*—being enslaved to a habit or practice or to a substance mentally or physically or both. Things start to change as the addiction grows. Once addicts start to worry about not being able to get their next hit, they become more selfish with their drugs. The obsession grows, and money becomes an issue. So, stealing and other criminal acts can start. Usually, addicts first start stealing from their families. Since parents don't want to believe it, they usually deny it until the situation is completely out of control. Then they might lock up their wallets, purses, and car keys, and put locks on their bedroom doors. So then, the addict might break and enter. A guy I knew once cooked up this elaborate scheme with his buddies to rob his own family's house and make it look like a "real" robbery!

Because the high or low you get from drugs is very strong, once you're hooked, it's got a hold on you that's very hard to break. You can't go without them, they're always on your mind, and everything else just stops mattering. You would do anything to get your next fix—even lie, cheat, steal, betray a friend, give up every last possession, hurt the people you love, sell yourself, hurt yourself, or even commit crimes—things you never imagined yourself doing. Drugs change who you are, your character, your morals and values.

Ryan With my brother, it reached a point where at times, I couldn't even recognize him. He would get really worked up over little things and lash out—he would scare me. Right before he died, I felt like we were strangers—I couldn't talk to him anymore, and he hardly ever spoke to me. My parents had no idea he was using, but their relationship had gone downhill too, and they knew something was terribly wrong. Drugs can destroy everything your family has worked hard to build—your home, your financial security, your community's respect. Not to mention, your parents might blame themselves or each other, thinking they failed you somehow. Talk about breaking people's hearts and tearing families apart.

Emile Even worse, I've seen addicts' poor attitudes and out-of-control behaviors get to the point where their own families would call the police or get them arrested because they didn't know how else to deal.

Startling facts

Drugs can be linked to
> Adolescent deaths
> Emergency room admissions
> Arrests

Ryan Yeah, arrest statistics go up when drugs are involved. So, you can get yourself locked up with a nice criminal record that will close a whole lot of doors in your face when it comes to your future and your chances in life. Colleges, employers, friends—nobody wants a criminal.

Emile Here's even more bad news: In 2003, marijuana was involved in 13 percent (79,663) of drug-related emergency room visits, and heroin was involved in 8 percent (47,604) of emergency room visits.[28] So, doing drugs is a pretty good way to end up in the hospital, and from the one time I've been there, I can tell you there are a whole lot of places I would

> In 2005, close to 1.4 million drivers were arrested for driving under the influence of alcohol or drugs. Drugs other than alcohol (e.g., marijuana and cocaine) are involved in about 18 percent of motor vehicle driver deaths. These other drugs are generally used in combination with alcohol.[29]

> In 2005, 4 percent of the 14,860 murders in which the reasons were known were drug related.[30]

> In 2004, an estimated 15,000 emergency room visits were the result of drug-related suicide attempts for people older than twelve.[31]

much rather be. Nothing fun about getting your stomach pumped or dying of a drug overdose. Thousands of kids didn't make it after using some kind of drug. Just like that, it was all over for them.

Eric Yeah. What people also don't realize is that drugs send your mind spinning in a bad way, and some make you jump out of your skin and become a danger to yourself and other people. But don't take my word for it: The statistics show drugs play a huge part in the three most common causes of death for teenagers—15,000 accidents, 6,000 homicides, and 5,000 suicides every year.

Ashley Wow! So, what are the specific side effects of different drugs, or are they basically all the same?

Emile Well, let's take marijuana—one everybody seems to think is no big deal.

Marijuana Use Side Effects
> Increased heart rate
> Red, bloodshot eyes
> Distorted sense of time, self, or reality
> Difficulty forming memories (could lead to permanent memory problems)
> Hallucinations, delusions, or learning or concentration problems
> Loss of personal identity
> Severe depression
> Anxiety, intense fear, or panic
> Problems with balance, posture, or coordination
> Lower testosterone levels and sperm count
> Dry mouth, extreme hunger or thirst
> Lower grades in school
> Problems on the job
> Damage to the immune system
> Destruction of brain cells

> Breathing problems
> Neck cancers[32]

Ashley So, how about other downers and the uppers?

Emile Well, downers really mess with your system in a big way, just like alcohol. Heroin is very, very addictive, both physically and mentally,[33] and it's got this powerful hold on you that you can't get past. It can throw you into *convulsions* (intense, involuntary contractions of the muscles in the body) and *seizures* (sudden attacks, spasms, or convulsions, just like in epilepsy).[34] If you take a larger dose than your body can handle, you can OD, and your heart can just stop. More overdosing deaths involve opiates—especially heroin—than any other drug.[35] The side effects of morphine and codeine are very similar when they're abused.

Heroin Use Side Effects
> Distorted sense of time, self, or reality
> Problems with balance, posture, or coordination
> Nausea and vomiting
> Build-up of fluids in the lungs (*pulmonary edema*)
> Destruction of brain cells
> Convulsions and seizures
> Breathing failure
> Heart failure
> Coma and death[36]

Ryan Cocaine is just as bad but in a different way. And cocaine can cause hallucinations, like "coke bugs," that make the person feel like bugs are crawling all over their body under their skin. Remember *The Mummy* movies?

Cocaine Use Side Effects
> Increased blood pressure, heart rate, breathing, and body temperature
> Immune system damage
> Brain seizures and stroke
> Hallucinations (e.g., "coke bugs") and delusions
> *Insomnia* (trouble sleeping)
> Psychosis
> Violent paranoia or aggression
> *Hepatitis* (inflammation of the liver) and even AIDS from contaminated needles
> Heart attack
> Death[37]

Eric Meth also has some huge and irreversible side effects.

Meth Use Side Effects
> Emotional numbness or feelings of being detached from others
> Anxiety, confusion, or insomnia
> Psychosis, paranoia, or mood swings
> Delusions and hallucinations
> Murder or suicidal thoughts
> Risky behavior because of increased sexual feelings
> Decreased appetite that can cause starvation or dehydration
> Damage to teeth and gums
> Burst blood vessels, skin sores, or lead poisoning
> Brain damage
> Breathing problems
> Seizures
> Heart attack
> Stroke
> Coma or death[38]

Karen And let me guess: Hallucinogen users can also die from the drugs too?

Eric You got it!

Emile Personally, I've only taken hallucinogens a couple of times, and the second time was bad, so I stopped them. But I've seen guys who took LSD on a regular basis freak out, get really violent, and go on a rampage. Or guys who imagine they're superheroes and can do things nobody else can do. This one time, a guy was so *strung out*—so high—he thought he could fly! Tried jumping out a fourth-floor window.

Hallucinogen Use Side Effects
> Distortion of the five senses
> Intense hallucinations or delusions
> Impaired mood, learning problems, and memory problems
> Feeling out of control
> Confusion, panic, anxiety, or psychosis
> *Night terrors* (bad dreams and flashbacks to a previous "trip")
> Violent and uncontrollable behavior
> Injury to self or others
> Dramatic increase in blood pressure, body temperature, and heart rate
> Sweating and dry mouth
> Tremors
> Huge pupils and bloodshot eyes

> Brain, heart, and lung damage
> Heart failure
> Brain seizures
> Coma or death[39]

Eric With over-the-counter or prescription drugs, depending on whether they're stimulants, depressants, or whatever, they can do any of the things we already talked about.

Over-the-Counter or Prescription Drug Use Side Effects
> Impaired judgment
> Loss of coordination
> Dizziness and nausea
> Hallucinations or delusions
> Paranoia or psychosis
> Damage to heart, brain, liver, kidneys, or other organs
> Coma and death[40]

Inhalants are pretty bad too. They can cause major side effects. And huffing only once can disrupt your heart rhythm and cause a deadly heart attack or stroke if the oxygen that goes to your lungs and brain gets cut off while you're huffing. It's called "sudden sniffing death."

Inhalant Use Side Effects
> Loss of inhibitions and impaired judgment
> Loss of balance and coordination
> Slurred speech
> Headaches
> Dizziness, nausea, and vomiting
> Anxiety or paranoia
> Hallucinations
> Wheezing and being out of breath
> Glue-sniffer's rash around the nose and mouth
> Memory problems
> Depression
> Permanent hearing loss
> Damage to nervous system and brain
> Damage to liver, kidneys, and heart
> Kidney abnormalities
> Heart attack or stroke—"sudden sniffing death"
> Heart failure
> Coma or death[41]

Karen And that date-rape drug, Rohypnol, and the others?

Date-Rape Drug Use Side Effects

GHB

> Drowsiness or dizziness
> Vision problems
> Hallucinations
> Increased heart rate
> Sweating
> Nausea and vomiting
> Breathing problems
> Blackouts
> *Amnesia* (memory loss or gaps)
> Paranoia or psychosis
> Coma and death

Rohypnol

> Distorted sense of time and space
> Loss of balance and coordination
> Drowsiness and confusion
> Vision problems
> Amnesia
> Vivid or disturbing dreams
> Irritability
> Short temper
> Hostility and aggression toward others

Ketamine

> Distorted sense of time and space
> Loss of balance and coordination
> Drowsiness and confusion
> Vision problems
> Hallucinations
> Loss of consciousness
> *K-hole*—near-death experience
> Severe amnesia
> Flashbacks and night terrors[42]

Ryan When a guy slips these drugs into a girl's drink, the girl loses her inhibitions and control. While she's under the influence of the drugs, the guy can rape her, and she can't even defend herself because she doesn't even know what's happening or she's completely passed out. Since the girl can't remember what happened, she can't accuse anyone of anything afterward.

Ashley Wow! That's so scary. What kind of person could do that to somebody else?

Ryan Well, a lot of the time, the guy is under the influence of alcohol or drugs himself and his judgment and values are way off too.

Keeping the Stash Stashed *Coping with or Covering Up Drug Use*

Emile Peer opinions are a pretty important thing when kids use drugs. If your friends don't use drugs and you know they won't approve, you'll deny it big time. You don't want people who care about you or look up to you to think you're a junkie, worry, or make a big deal over it. And if you are abusing drugs, you don't want anything to mess with getting your next fix. That means lying and denying—making sure everybody buys your stories and doesn't suspect a thing. So, you get really good at making up excuses about where you are when you disappear, what you're doing when your bathroom door is locked, why your stuff's gone missing, why your eyes are bloodshot, and why you look out of it or just plain sick.

Ryan Addicts do a lot to pull the wool over people's eyes, like drinking coffee to wake up when they've been doing downers, sleeping all weekend after finally crashing from uppers, spraying air freshener or opening windows a lot, or making up really creative excuses about why they're failing at school or lagging behind on the football field. If they get caught with drugs, they might say they're just "holding them for a friend" and on and on. Drug addicts can write the book on excuses. It's easy to fool people. My brother did for a long time.

Emile Little by little, the signs get harder to miss and people stop buying your stories. So, drug users often start avoiding people who are not part of that lifestyle and surround themselves with people who are okay with drugs. First, that helps them avoid disapproving glances and conflict. Second, hanging with other people who "party" puts them closer to the source of supply, so their next hit is for sure. People who use always have some extra stuff stashed around. So, if you run out of drugs or money to buy them, others will hook you up. Also, you compare your drug use to the other people's and you can comfort yourself with, "His use is *way* worse than mine." It helps you minimize and deny to yourself how serious your problem is. Sooner or later, all the people who were part of your "old" life when you didn't use fall by the wayside—your junkie friends become your new clique.

Eric Unfortunately, this thinking only supports your drug use, because you're only around other people who do drugs. You believe your behavior is normal. You get trapped in this make-believe reality.

Ryan Even people who have only taken drugs once in a while aren't the best at handling it and balancing their lives. Drugs distract you from the other things in your life. You start losing track of responsibilities like school, homework, tests, extracurricular activities, and promises to people. Or you might become really hyper and energetic and get a lot done, but then lose steam when you come off your high and end up crashing, which makes you unreliable and unpredictable. Your mood could change quickly, and that turns people off too and makes them not want to be around you.

Emile Not to mention, when you're acting all weird and losing focus at school, your teachers might figure it out. So, you could get suspended or expelled. And your entire life and future get that much harder overnight.

Karen And if your parents find out, they might lose trust in you, especially if things go missing in the house. You become distant from the people who make the greatest difference in your life and are your biggest supporters. Some kids end up running away from home because they can't stand to see the disappointment or live by the rules. Your family becomes the enemy—the people who are standing between you and the habit.

Emile If you run away from home, chances are you don't have tons of money in your pocket. And if you shack up with your new "friends"—other junkies—they won't let you get a free ride forever. You'll have to "pay your dues" and bring in some drugs. The catch is, the more drugs you do, the less you're able to do anything else—including hold a job. So, you aren't working, but you need money for drugs. You gotta get it somewhere. This is when petty theft, muggings, or holding up mini-marts start to sound like good ideas. Especially if you are an addict—then you will do just about anything. You might even start selling drugs, stealing cars, shoplifting, even prostitution or hurting people. All of a sudden, you're a criminal.

Ryan Unfortunately, not everyone sees addiction as the disease that it is. The public mainly sees it as a sign of weakness and a behavior problem. So, there's little motivation for an addict to admit they have a problem. Society considers them delinquents, and nobody wants to be seen as a low-life. Add to that the fact that, most of the time, the drug abuser is in denial about the problem, and you have a nasty combination.

If drug users *do* recognize and admit they're in trouble, which is rare, they could feel very guilty, angry, or sad. They might think they don't deserve anything good or feel helpless to fix the problem. They might become so depressed, hopeless, resigned, or indifferent that they stop caring about their life and safety. They could become really careless about danger and even put themselves in harm's way on purpose.

Emile Some people might even go so far as to kill themselves. I knew this guy who used to buy his heroin from one of the kids I ran with. He came from a really good, wealthy family, but he was a hard-core addict. The heroin was killing him. He knew it. He had been to rehab three times, and every time he started up again. I remember asking him one night how he could keep using knowing what it was doing to him. He said he just couldn't stop, and he wished he could just OD one day and it could be over. A couple of days later, my friend told me he had over-dosed and died. I think he did it on purpose.

Ryan If you finally do get caught and cornered, you might admit what's going on and make promises to others that you will change or stop. Drug

Coping or Cover-Up Techniques Drug Users or Addicts Use
❯ Lying, sneaking around, or denying there's anything wrong
❯ Making a lot of excuses
❯ Skipping school or dropping the ball on activities, responsibilities, or promises to others
❯ Burning incense or spraying air freshener all the time
❯ Locking themselves in their room or bathroom a lot
❯ Withdrawing or distancing themselves from their friends and loved ones
❯ Hanging out with a different crowd that does drugs
❯ Selling valuables that belong to them or their family to score money for drugs
❯ Destroying relationships with their family
❯ Quitting school, quitting their job, or running away
❯ Getting into risky or criminal things to score money for drugs
❯ Fessing up and making promises to clean up and stop doing drugs
❯ Recognizing their problem and being ready to get treatment

I've Got This Friend Who...

users make promises all the time but usually don't keep them. They often can't, even when they want to. Remember: Deep down, drug addicts are "brainwashed"—they're under a drug's spell. They figure if they say all the right things, people will believe them and get off their back. It's rare when drug addicts are truly *ready* to change.

Emile If they're pushed and given no other choice, they might go for help. Once they're there, the treatment can work even if they aren't convinced they want it, but they have to at least go.

Eye-Popping Tip-Offs *Warning Signs That Your Friend Is Using Drugs or That You're in Too Deep*

Ryan It is very important to know what to look for, so we can spot if loved ones are abusing drugs or if we're in too deep.

Eric There are some really obvious warning signs. First off, if you know somebody really well, anything that seems out of character or looks suspicious should tip you off. Like, if they're always a pretty patient and kind person, and all of a sudden, they're snapping at everybody—bull's-eye! Other things like people disappearing often and not telling you where they were or what they were doing are clues too. So is shutting you out, avoiding you, or completely changing their group of friends. Getting caught with drugs or doing something else illegal and being in trouble with the law is also eye-opening. Money might go missing from other people's wallets and purses when that person is around, or their stuff (like an iPod, Xbox, or jewelry) might always "get lost" or "stolen."

Karen Another really good sign is when people completely lose interest in the things that used to matter—like doing well in school, a certain sport, a favorite hobby, or friends and loved ones. Pay attention if you catch them in lies a lot, or if they act weird and always run off, sneak around, or are secretive.

Eric If they miss curfew, become apathetic, skip school, withdraw from their family, or run away, these are also signs.

Karen And what if *you* personally start experimenting with drugs? What if I tried a drug—which I didn't, but let's pretend I did. What kinds of questions can I ask myself to figure out if I'm getting in too deep or I'm already hooked?

A user might	You might find
› Lose weight quickly	› Cigarette rolling papers or other small pieces of paper
› Become apathetic and lose interest in the things and people that mattered	› Pipes
› Go "missing" a lot and always have lots of excuses about where she was	› Bongs
› Miss curfew or skip school	› Homemade smoking devices
› Hang out with people who do drugs	› Injection marks on her skin
› Steal or commit other crimes like selling drugs, hurting people, or even selling herself	› Money or valuables missing
› Run away	› Burnt spoons
› Neglect her appearance	› Small unmarked pills of different shapes, sizes, and colors
› Have bad breath	› Small bottles of white powder
› Burn incense a lot	› Lots of bottles of prescription medications
› Lock herself in her room or bathroom often	› Empty aerosol cans
› Leave windows open or spray air freshener often	› Containers of glue, nail polish, marker pens, or correction fluid
› Complain her skin burns or itches	› Butane lighters
› Have constricted pupils, watery eyes, and droopy eyelids	› Strong gasoline or solvent smell
› Have bloodshot eyes	› Razor blades
› Have enlarged pupils, sweat excessively, or smell bad	› Mirrors
› Seem anxious or afraid of a lot of things that don't make sense	› Straws
› Have paint stains on her body, face, or clothes	
› Frequently sneeze or cough	
› Have a runny nose or nosebleeds often	
› Slur her speech	
› Be very restless and talkative, but have nothing of importance to say and jump from topic to topic without any connection	
› Look through medicine cabinets a lot	
› Have nightmares a lot	
› Have major mood swings often—including being irritable, being short-tempered, flying off the handle easily, and being violent	
› Lie, deny, or make lots of excuses	
› Withdraw or distance herself from loved ones and friends	
› Have unexplained valuables go missing	
› Have money or other valuables from other people's purses or houses go missing when she's around	

Emile That's a really good question. Here are the basic statements my drug abuse counselors at rehab say will give you a reality check:

You May Have a Problem with Drugs if You...
› Are worried you may have a problem
› Can't predict whether you will get high
› Believe that you need to get high to have fun

- Turn to drugs after a confrontation or argument, or to relieve uncomfortable feelings
- Use more drugs to get the same effect that you got with smaller amounts before
- Do drugs alone
- Remember how last night began, but not how it ended
- Have trouble at school because of getting high or being high in class
- Have angry outbursts, do risky things, or become violent with other people
- Make and break promises to yourself or others that you'll stop doing drugs
- Feel that you need the drug regularly just to get through the day
- Feel alone, scared, miserable, and depressed without drugs
- No longer spend time with friends who don't use drugs
- Keep company mostly with people who use drugs
- Steal money or other things from other people or sell your prized possessions to buy drugs
- Do dangerous or illegal things to get money for drugs
- Constantly think about your next fix, talk about drugs all the time, and even pressure others to use with you
- Are willing to do just about anything to get drugs
- Stop caring about the things that used to matter and feel as if nothing else matters but the drugs

Knowledge Is Power *Preventing Yourself or a Friend from Giving In to the Hype about Drugs*

Ryan Know what I think the biggest problem is? Not enough kids and teens actually know all of the really horrible things that can happen if they do get caught up in drugs.

Emile You got that right. The guys I knew definitely didn't. I think they thought it would be this wild ride, when the reality is it was a crash-landing for many of them!

Ryan Right. So, the most important thing to do is learn all you can about the drugs out there and educate your friends and loved ones. That way, you'll know where you might come across the stuff and how to be ready to say "no" if you're faced with the choice or the pressure.

If you ask me, the education needs to start really early—in elementary school. Kids that age are eager to learn everything about everything, so it's a perfect time to influence a younger brother's or sister's decision about drugs in a positive way. All you guys who have younger siblings, they look up to you and care about what you think and have to say. I know I did. You're their heroes. And you are closer to their age than any adult. So, you can make a big difference in their choices.

Jessica Well, how do you bring up the subject with younger kids?

Karen You should make it simple and be casual—you don't want to scare them off. Then, as the conversation gets going, you can build up to more serious stuff. Always keep the lines of communication open and don't be judgmental. Be understanding, open-minded, and caring—be a pal.

Emile If you're talking about teaching other kids from the get-go or even talking to friends your age about it, there are a few things you want to make sure they get.

Things to Say to Your Friends and Siblings about Drugs

"*You don't have to do drugs to be cool*—whether it is pot, triple C, inhalants, or any other drug."

"*You don't have to do drugs to have a good time*—you can get just as 'high' spending time with people you care about, pursuing a talent or a hobby, doing really well at something, playing sports, or doing other things that give you a sense of purpose and make you feel good about yourself."

"*Using any drug in any amount doesn't make you more masculine, feminine, grown-up, or attractive.* It just makes you more vulnerable and less in control."

"*Drugs are really dangerous* and can make really bad things happen to your mind and your body that can get you badly hurt or even killed."

"*Friends and relatives that use or abuse drugs* are in trouble and need help; *you shouldn't try to be like them.*"

"*Being 'stoned,' 'messed up,' or 'coked up' is not funny,* and if you laugh at someone who is, you're giving them the wrong message: that it's no big deal, and you basically approve of their behavior."

"*Doing drugs to feel better* when you're feeling bad or having a hard time with something *is not a solution. It is only a temporary fix.* After the high wears off, you still have the same problem you had before plus another problem to worry about—the drugs."

"*If you're confused* about how you feel about something or what to do, *come talk to me.* I don't have all the answers, but I might have some. Hey, you might even have some answers for me! We can teach each other and keep each other out of trouble—I will if you will!"

"*Say 'no' to drugs* and 'yes' to your life!"

One Word Can Save Your Life
Learning to Say "No" to Drugs

Ashley Well, it's one thing to know the facts—it's quite another thing to say "no" when someone pressures you to try drugs, especially if they're part of a group you're dying to be part of. No one likes being left out, and if you say "no," it could happen.

Karen Just being at a party or anyplace where there are drugs puts you in a position to have to make that choice. So, it *is* a good idea to know how to refuse without losing face. One good way is to blame it on other people.

Ryan For me it's the same thing as with alcohol—I've used the sports excuse a lot.

Jessica I've used some excuses before too, believe it or not, like being sick.

Emile You could always be a smart-mouth and "dis" the person with something clever.

Eric Or if worse comes to worst, you could take the pill or whatever and excuse yourself—go to the bathroom and flush it down the toilet, like with liquor. What are the chances others would follow you to the toilet bowl?

You don't always have to give an explanation for saying "no." But if you feel you have to, there are a bunch you can use.

What to Say If Someone Pressures You to Do Drugs or to Get into a Car with a Driver Who's High

"No, thanks. I don't do drugs."

"My parents are coming to pick me up soon, and if they smelled pot on me, I'd be grounded for sure!"

"My uncle is in recovery and would be so disappointed if I got into trouble for using drugs."

"I have a game tomorrow," or "I have an early practice in the morning."

"Sorry, I don't feel well tonight; I'll sit this one out."

"Sorry, pot or coke (or whatever) is not my thing."

"Gee, I have better things to do, like staying alive."

"I know you're not the sharpest tool in the shed, but it's just two letters: N.O. Take your time with that one—no rush."

"Sorry, I'm allergic to drugs."

"No thanks, I've got a ride."

"I think I'm gonna walk—I'm only a few blocks away."

"I made a New Year's resolution to only ride with drivers who are high on life."

Ryan The point is, there are plenty of things to say besides "No, thanks, I don't do drugs," which is also an option if you're not afraid to be an independent thinker and stand up for being drug free. Ever since my brother's death in the car accident, I've had no problem saying that straight up.

Jessica And what about the date-rape drugs? You've got me all freaked out. You don't even have, like, the choice to say "no." Someone could just drop it in your drink when you aren't looking.

Karen I can't believe there are guys like that out there. Scum! Girls, sounds like we gotta stick together. You know, don't accept drinks from anyone except your friends and keep your drinks with you even if you go to the bathroom. And if you do leave a drink, don't come back and drink it. Don't drink other people's drinks or anything from a large shared container, like a punch bowl or keg.

Also, we need to be responsible and look out for each other. We have to know where our friends are at all times and make sure they're okay. Keep an eye on the people you came with. If a friend is acting like she had way too much to drink and doesn't know what's going on—especially if you didn't see her having any alcohol or having that much—stay close to her and don't let anybody drag her off somewhere. The best thing to do is just take her home right away.

Jessica But what if we try all that and something still happens? Sometimes parties get real crowded, and you're bumping into people, and you never know what can happen.

Ryan In the worst case, if you don't remember a part of the night and you suspect something did happen, tell someone right away! Go to the police or a hospital and ask for drug screening...and a rape test!

Eric Don't wait—get the drug test as soon as possible. I read that date-rape drugs get broken down and thrown out of the body real fast, so sometimes, there's no evidence twelve hours after you take them.

Ashley Good advice! What else?

Handy tip

Before you get to a party or go out for the evening, you and your friends should set up a signal to let each other know if you want to leave or if you need help.

Karen Well, sometimes, my friends and I set things up beforehand. Like, we'll decide on a signal to give each other when we want to leave or when we're being hassled and need help. Friends can back you up or create a distraction to help get you out of that situation. Like, if you see somebody hassling your friend about doing drugs, just jump in with some bogus story and interrupt the conversation. It works!

Ashley Cool! Sounds like the best thing to do is to plan ahead and be ready.

Karen You can also learn to avoid situations where you know drugs are gonna be passed around. Learn your lesson the first time and don't go back to the same places where you know kids are up to no good. If there's a person whose parties always involve drugs, just don't go there. Or if a certain group is always partying like that, keep your distance. When you're with your friends, find fun, exciting things to do instead of just sitting around. Go to the mall, go skating, go bowling, or play a volleyball game. That keeps you busy, so you don't need to turn to drugs out of boredom.

Taking a "Crack" at Drugs
Loosening the Chokehold on Your Life or Your Friend's Life

Ashley What if it's too late? What if you've already, like, stepped over the edge or if one of your friends has gone down that road?

Emile Well, if you or they are just starting to experiment and it's still a curiosity thing, cut your losses and stop while you still can. Start avoiding the people and places where drugs get passed around. Or if you absolutely can't cut yourself off, use the things we just talked about to say "no." But my advice is: Bail before you get sucked in! If you cut the influence off at the pass, you'll have a better chance of staying drug free. So, find other things, like talents, hobbies, or other activities that give you a natural high, make you feel good, and give you the chance to make friends who don't do drugs.

Jessica And if you're already in too deep? Like, if you're already using drugs on a regular basis or abusing them? Or if you're afraid a friend, cousin, brother, sister, teammate, whoever is—then what?

Emile Well, I'm not gonna lie to you. Doing nothing is not an option. If you keep using drugs, they *will* kill you—sooner or later. And in the meantime, they will destroy everything you care about—your family, your relationships, your opportunities, your future, your hopes and dreams, your entire life. Addiction is a serious illness, and you need to get treated to get better.

And it takes time. The addiction didn't happen overnight, and the recovery definitely won't. Trust me on that one. After all, drugs cause actual changes in how your mind and body work, so it takes awhile to change them back to the way they were before. Addiction affects how people act too, so it takes time to undo those bad habits.

Karen So, if you are in trouble, the important thing is to ask for help!

Ryan If it's your friend we're talking about, arm yourself with all kinds of information so you know what you're talking about. Once you decide to say something, prepare yourself with a list of specific things you want to talk about—like how his drug use is harming him and other people around him. Make sure the person knows how much you care. And remember: The goal is to get him to take some positive action against his drug use.

Emile There's that method I mentioned when we talked about drinking called Share Your Concern.[43] Basically, you use a bunch of statements that help you with a difficult talk.

Share Your Concern

I CARE You tell the person you care and that you are concerned, how much his friendship means to you, and how important he is in your life.

I SEE You explain to him exactly what you saw him do that made you worry. (For example, you could say, "Last night at the party, you took several different pills, and you started acting out of control.")

I FEEL You tell him how it makes you feel when he acts like that. (For example, you could say, "I'm worried because I've known you since first grade, and that isn't you.")

LISTEN You give him the chance to say what's on his mind or ask questions. This is the time to really listen and show him you care about whatever he says. No matter how upset or angry he becomes, you need to remain calm, stay focused, and avoid judging.

I WANT You tell him what you want to see happen. (For example, you could say, "I want you to talk to someone about the drugs and how you act when you're high.")

I WILL You tell him how you will support him and what you're willing to do to help. Again, you continue to tell him how much you care. (For example, you could say, "I really care about you, and I will help you find someone who can help you. I will go to the guidance counselor with you. You are my friend, and I am here for you.")

Like with alcohol, it a great first step, but it's still a confrontation, regardless of how much you plan. So, it might not go totally smoothly. Your friend might freak out on you, get really defensive, get angry, or just stomp out of the room. Drug users aren't usually ready or willing to hear the ugly truth. Prepare yourself for that. And remember, whatever your friend says to you, it's not her, it's the drugs talking. So, don't take it personally. The important thing is to be realistic, optimistic, and supportive. Expect the worst but also hope for the best. Give your friend a chance to think about it, and keep the door open if she wants to talk again.

Jessica Okay, so let's say, for argument's sake, that it works. She agrees to get help. Then what?

Eric The most important step to solving a problem is admitting there is one. So, you've won half the battle. Now comes the harder part—helping your friend get help.

Karen Whether it's you or your friend that has a problem, you can start with parents. They are your first line of defense against the world, so if they're caring and involved, no matter how upset they are, they will definitely want to help. You could also go to a counselor, a family friend, a favorite coach or teacher, or even a minister if you're too afraid or ashamed to go to a parent.

If you don't want to start there, you can call a local drug and alcohol support program like Narcotics Anonymous, or a therapist, outpatient clinic, or drug rehab center to learn how you can sign up. There are also Web sites you can check out.

Emile People always think they have to give up their lives and "go away" to get treated. Yes, that's one option, but there are other treatment options.

Treatment Options

Outpatient treatment The person attends at least weekly counseling sessions with a therapist who specializes in addiction or prevention of drug use.

Intensive outpatient treatment (IOP) The person attends several counseling sessions per week, with different focuses: individual counseling, group counseling, and family counseling.

Partial hospitalization (PH) Treatment and counseling are provided in a medical environment or hospital while the patient still lives at home. Counseling takes place every day, and if the person has other problems, like depression, anger, or a mood disorder, a psychiatrist might get involved too. So, the treatment is more intensive and more concentrated than in traditional outpatient care.

A treatment facility The person goes here if he can't get past the drug addiction and needs to move into a place where patients live and are treated full time. The two options are a *drug and alcohol facility* or a *dual diagnosis facility*, which allows both drug addiction and mental health issues to be treated together, since they often go hand in hand.

Beating the Odds *Staying Clean*

Karen Is there ever any downside of treatment? I mean, can anything bad or unpleasant happen?

Eric Well, yeah, once you stop using drugs, everything feels less intense. It's disappointing to you. So, there's a huge temptation to *relapse*—to go back to using the substance after quitting—once you get out of rehab. It's real easy to get sucked back in when doctors and your support group aren't looking over your shoulder. The statistics vary, but it seems like a lot of people relapse. In 2002, about 1.9 million people were admitted to substance abuse treatment centers. Forty-four percent were first-time admissions, 45 percent had one to four previous treatments, and 11 percent had five or more previous treatments![44]
Sometimes recovering addicts go through *withdrawal* too, like with alcohol. They have all these really unpleasant physical or mental symptoms that happen when they stop using the drugs. They may have overwhelming cravings or bad feelings. People who stop taking coke could feel really depressed, anxious, or antsy. They might have bad dreams, have trouble sleeping, eat like crazy, or not be able to feel pleasure from anything. Other people actually physically feel pain or have a fever, seizures, or delusions. Withdrawal from heroin and meth is particularly hard and painful.

Ryan Well, correct me if I'm wrong, but the temptation to relapse will be much stronger if you go back to your old familiar hangouts where you used to do drugs or you meet up with your buddies who still do them.

Emile For sure! That's why I always tell people to cut the cord. You can't go back to doing what you used to do before you went into rehab. You have to stay away from the people who fed your habit and got you into drugs in the first place. It's important to identify high-risk situations, so you can avoid them or prepare to work through them. You gotta close that door and open a new one—one where you do other stuff besides drugs that makes you feel good and gets your blood pumping.

You can remind yourself or your friend that the stakes are high. Just imagine the consequences of a relapse! Would it really be worth it? You can also remind your friends you're in recovery and ask them to respect your goal.

Karen But what if your friends not only continue to use themselves, but push you to do the same?

Finding the Strength to Stick to It

▶ Remind yourself abstinence is the goal.

▶ Remind yourself the stakes are high.

▶ Remind your friends you're in recovery and need them to be sensitive and supportive.

▶ Consider Twelve Step self-help groups where you can feel accepted and experience the tolerance you need.

▶ Meet new people with common healthy interests and goals to help keep you on track.

▶ Learn to enjoy the natural high you can get from good relationships.

▶ Know your triggers—it helps you to plan ahead.

▶ Identify high-risk situations and be ready to avoid them.

▶ Develop coping skills and interests by pursuing a passion or hobby to enhance your self-esteem, promote your personal development, and replace your addiction. Examples include music, reading, writing, sports, or a peer group.

▶ Work with a counselor who can provide the guidance and trusting relationship you need to keep going.

▶ Get professional psychiatric help to help you explore the underlying or complicating issues around your drug abuse. Psychiatrists will also be able to prescribe legitimate and helpful medications for other issues, such as emotional problems.

▶ Express your feelings or urges to a friend, counselor, or your Narcotics Anonymous sponsor.

▶ Make yourself the "designated driver" for your friends.

▶ Take credit for the "wellbriety" (being *well* and *sober*) that comes with all your hard work.

▶ Don't blame yourself or be discouraged if you relapse, but rather use relapses as learning experiences to find your weaknesses and as stepping stones for future success.

Ryan Sounds to me like it would be time to find new friends—ones that are clean, healthy and pro-recovery. Meet new people and learn to enjoy the natural highs that come from good relationships or success in school and other fun stuff.

Eric You can also learn to cope by expressing your feelings to your friends or counselor, or by calling your Narcotics Anonymous (NA) sponsor for support if you're really tempted. If you're on medication, you can also remind yourself that drugs and meds don't mix. And you can be a designated driver. That way, you have the perfect excuse to not use.

Where to Get Help

Emile When it comes to drugs, there are so many places to look for help. The 125-year-old national children's organization KidsPeace has information on its Web site. There are a bunch of other organizations and Web sites that are really helpful too. Don't wait—get help now.

Web Sites

KidsPeace
www.KidsPeace.org
The Web site of the 125-year-old children's charity contains information about all the popular street drugs and their effects.

TeenCentral.Net
www.TeenCentral.Net
This Web site by the children's charity KidsPeace is especially designed for teens and offers anonymous, free, clinically screened advice to help you deal with the problems you face every day, so you can avoid turning to drugs for comfort.

Students Against Destructive Decisions
www.sadd.org
This teen peer organization Web site helps teens join together in saying "no" to drugs and lots of other destructive choices.

Partnership for a Drug-Free America
www.drugfree.org
This Web site has a section for teens that helps you learn more about drugs, their dangers, real life stories, and how to get help if you're in too deep.

Narcotics Anonymous
www.na.org

The Web site of the international drug recovery support network gives you information about support groups and meetings across the world, as well as related events and news that can help you kick the habit.

National Institute on Drug Abuse
www.drugabuse.gov, www.sarasquest.org

These Web sites—the organization's main Web site and its special Web site for teens—give you all the facts about the most popular street drugs, the science behind addiction, and the consequences to empower you to make educated, smart choices.

Office of National Drug Control Policy
www.whitehousedrugpolicy.gov

This Web site of the government's efforts against drugs gives you detailed information about the making, trafficking, selling, and use of drugs; their dangers; and drug-related crime and violence to help you stay drug-free.

Hotlines

Cocaine/Crack Helpline
1-800-COCAINE (1-800-262-2463, 24 hours; referrals to treatment programs)

Cocaine Anonymous
1-800-347-8998 (international referral line; links to local meetings)

Marijuana Anonymous
1-800-766-6779 (links to local meetings)

National Clearinghouse for Alcohol and Drug Information
1-800-729-6686 (English information and referral)
1-877-767-8432 (Spanish information and referral)

Additional Resources

Web Sites

National Clearinghouse for Alcohol and Drug Information, the U.S. Department of Health and Human Services, Substance Abuse and Mental Health Services Administration
http://ncadi.samhsa.gov

National Institute on Drug Abuse, National Institutes of Health (NIH)
www.nida.nih.gov

Teen Web Site, National Institute on Drug Abuse, NIH
http://teens.drugabuse.gov/

Teen Web Page on Drugs, American Academy of Child & Adolescent Psychiatry
http://aacap.org/cs/root/facts_for_families/teens_alcohol_and_other_drugs

Books

From Binge to Blackout: A Mother and Son Struggle with Teen Drinking by Chris Volkmann and Toren Volkmann

A Teen's Guide to Living Drug-Free by Bettie B. Youngs, Jennifer Leigh Youngs, and Tina Moreno

Drugs 101: An Overview for Teens by Margaret O. Hyde and John F. Setaro, M.D.

The Original Drug Manual for Kids and Families by J.T. Barrie

Chicken Soup for the Kid's Soul: 101 Stories of Courage, Hope and Laughter by Jack Canfield, Mark Victor Hansen, Patty Hansen, and Irene Dunlap

What We Can't Tell You: Teenagers Talk to the Adults in Their Lives by Kathleen Cushman and the youth of What Kids Can Do

My Big Sister Takes Drugs by Judith Vigna

Drugs in Perspective: A Personalized Look at Substance Use and Abuse by Richard Fields

Dirty: A Search for Answers Inside America's Teenage Drug Epidemic by Meredith Maran

The Cocaine Kids: The Inside Story of a Teenage Drug Ring by Terry M. Williams

The O'Reilly Factor for Kids: A Survival Guide for America's Families by Bill O'Reilly and Charles Flowers

Cool Parents, Drug-Free Kids: A Family Survival Guide by Robert Holman Coombs

People need to eat to live. Food is the fuel that runs our bodies. It's a means of survival in some cultures, an indulgence in others, an opportunity to socialize and bond with family and friends in others—but certainly a necessity in all. Unfortunately, sometimes people develop unhealthy relationships with food, and eating can get out of control. Bad eating habits based on the wrong reasons for eating and wrong ways of eating can cause eating disorders.

An eating disorder is an abnormal combination of eating habits, feelings about food and weight, and methods of weight control. Eating disorders affect both a person's physical and mental health. They're happening more and more, especially to young people, who are caught up in a vicious cycle of trying to attain the "perfect" body. There's no such thing, of course, and often their quest ends in tragedy. The devastating consequences wreak havoc in the lives of many kids and teens and are also felt by their families, friends, and all the people who love them.

—*Jana Hill, R.D., L.D.N., C.D.E.*

We're constantly bombarded by images of tall, skinny, fit, beautiful people who set the standard for what's attractive, appreciated, and desirable. The media glorify the "perfect" body constantly and seem to be sending the loud and clear message that anything less just won't do. Dolls and action figures also set an example for kids from a very early age of what a man or woman should look like. The standards our society sets on physical appearance are often impossible to achieve, as magazine photos are airbrushed, movies are digitally enhanced, and dolls and action figures come in proportions that the human body can never reach.

For a young person living in a culture obsessed with dieting and thinness, it may be very difficult to navigate all the unrealistic expectations and build a healthy body image. It is also hard to know when your thinking about food or eating has become a problem. Eating disorders, just like the people who suffer from them, are different. They may be very severe and visible or very subtle, creeping into your life almost unnoticed. If unchecked, they can have lasting and tragic results.

—**Annita B. Jones, Psy.D.**

Ashley

A RECIPE FOR DISASTER

The Terrible Truth about Eating Disorders and How to Stop before Your Goose Gets Cooked

Jessica   Eric   Karen   Emile   Ryan

Eating *The Good, the Bad, the Ugly*

Karen Before we get started for today, anyone want a brownie? My mom baked them.

Ryan Sure—thanks!

Emile You know I'd never turn down brownies!

Eric They *are* awesome!

Jessica I'll try a really small one...mmmm, yummy!

Karen Ash? How 'bout you?

Ashley Uh...no. No, thanks.

Emile Why, Ash? Don't tell me—you're trying to lose weight?

Ashley Well, staying thin is really important! You know, I want to look good so people will like me. Especially now that I'm in high school. Besides, there's nothing wrong with being thin—better than being fat.

Karen Nobody's saying you should be fat, Ash, but first off, you are plenty thin. Second, it's not just fat and thin. There are other levels of weight in between, you know. And third, it's not the only thing people notice about you. You have a great personality, you're smart, you're funny. What's not to like about you?

Jessica Yeah, maybe in *your* world that's enough. But not if you want to be part of the in-crowd. And not to sound shallow, but we all think looks are important. The in-crowd is just not afraid to be, like, up-front about it.

Karen Well, that can't be the *only* thing you all think is important!

Jessica No, not the *only* thing, but it's a big thing—it's basically, like, the first impression. The first thing people notice about you.

Karen Yeah, well, I don't get that whole thing. I mean, you don't have to be a size zero to be beautiful and everyone else is a whale. I have a ton of friends, and we never worry about how skinny we are, or if we have an off day and don't look our best, or if our makeup is not all perfect.

Jessica Yeah, but that whole "alternative" thing works for you.

Karen Yeah, and I'm perfectly happy! My friends and I think there's a lot more to life than someone's looks.

Jessica I didn't mean it as an insult. All I'm saying is there are different expectations for different social groups. And to fit in, you have to fit those expectations.

Karen Yeah, well, that whole thing about expectations gets me really worked up. Our society is totally obsessed with looks and the "perfect" body, whatever that means. Everywhere you look, you see images of barely dressed, skin-and-bones, overly primped, made-up celebrities showing off their bodies. What they don't tell you is all the makeup and hair time, airbrushing, digital tricks, and different camera angles that make those images of celebs look perfect. It's totally bogus!

Ashley Well, some pop stars who are our age *are* actually pretty skinny and *do* actually look amazing! It's not always the airbrushing and the digital tricks. And it's not just the female teen idols, either. Look at, like, male models. They're thin, cut, and...perfect! No wonder kids put all this pressure on themselves.

Eric On top of that, the dolls and action figures we play with as kids— they also teach us from a very early age what we want to look like when we grow up. But I read that, actually, their proportions are impossible for the human body to *ever* come close to, no matter how much you starve, exercise, body build, or even do risky things like surgeries.

Ryan People come in all shapes and sizes. Some kids have bigger, heavier bones, but others' bone structures are much smaller and lighter. Some girls are bustier than others. Some guys have more muscles than others. Your family genes make a difference. And also, some people's metabolism is much faster than others'. Your *metabolic rate* is how fast your body breaks down and burns food.[1] That's why some people can eat a horse and stay skinny and others eat a cup of yogurt and gain weight.

Eric Right. Also, listen to this: The average woman is five foot four and 164 pounds. The average man is five foot nine-and-a-half and 191 pounds,[2] which is not even close to the ideal out there.

Karen Well, everybody seems to be feeding into the hype. We're a nation obsessed with weight and dieting. You read articles on new fad diets and weight-loss tips all the time. It rubs off on kids big time. I read this report that said like only 18 percent of grade-school girls have a positive-enough body image that they don't think they need to model themselves after today's ultra-thin celebrities.[3] Can you believe that?

Jessica You make it sound like I should feel guilty for watching my weight...or liking people who are thin.

Karen Nothing wrong with being weight and health conscious, Jess. As long as it's in moderation and takes into account what Eric brought up. I'm five foot four, and no matter how skinny I get, I'm never gonna look like a five-foot-nine supermodel. And you should also watch your weight for the right reasons—health reasons—not for looks and trying to live up to an impossible standard.

Eric When it's weight watching gone berserk, it isn't a good thing. The fact is, your body needs nutritious food from all five food groups and a certain number of calories per day to keep you going. *Calories* are units of energy contained in food.[7] Pure and simple, we all need to eat right to keep our bodies running.

Metabolic rate
how fast your body breaks down and burns food

Body basics
What your body is like all depends on biology, genetics, body structure, bone size and weight, and metabolism.

Startling facts
Weight watching gone nuts:
- 40 to 60 percent of high school girls diet[4]
- 30 to 40 percent of junior high girls worry about their weight[5]
- 81 percent of ten-year-old girls have dieted before[6]

Eating Disorders *Biting Off More Than You Can Chew*

Eating disorder
a combination of
eating habits, feelings
about food and
weight, and ways
of weight control
that are not normal
or healthy. Eating
disorders are serious!

**Anorexia
(anorexia nervosa)**
a serious, often
chronic, and life-
threatening eating
disorder, characterized
by body image
distortions and an
obsession with being
thin that involves
starving yourself or
depriving yourself of
food on a regular basis

**Bulimia
(bulimia nervosa)**
a serious, often
chronic, and life-
threatening eating
disorder that involves
binging, which is
eating a huge amount
of food at one time,
and then intentional
purging, which is
getting rid of the food
in some way

Ryan That's so true. And when people start changing their eating habits drastically and in unhealthy ways, it could be trouble. You can develop what's called an *eating disorder*, which is a combination of eating habits, feelings about food and weight, and ways of weight control that are not normal or healthy.

Karen It's important that we all understand the different types of eating disorders. First there's *anorexia* or *anorexia nervosa*, characterized by body image distortions and an obsession with being thin.

Even though they're often too thin, people who are anorexic think they look fat. They usually won't let on to anyone that they're hungry and act like they don't feel like eating, but actually, they're starving, literally. Anorexia could threaten your life.[8]

Emile Don't people with an eating disorder make themselves throw up?

Karen That's another type of eating disorder—*bulimia nervosa*. It involves *binging,* eating a huge amount of food at one time, and then *purging,* getting rid of it in some way.

Bulimics purge by forcing themselves to throw up, overexercising, or using a lot of laxatives or diuretics. *Laxatives* are pills or other chemicals that relieve constipation and can cause diarrhea, and *diuretics* are pills or chemicals that make you have to pee. I read a bulimic could eat up to 20,000 calories at one time—like eating three chocolate, seven-layer cakes in one shot—and then purge to "undo" it.[9]

Eric Anorexia and bulimia are the eating disorders people know best. But there's also *compulsive overeating,* or *binge eating disorder,* which is pretty much the opposite thing. It involves eating huge quantities of food without purging.

Usually, this eating disorder starts when people are really young. Some kids find food comforting, so they'll eat to deal with bad situations and make themselves feel better. Or to "stuff away" the bad or uncomfortable feelings. Afterward, they feel guilty, disgusted with themselves, and depressed. They usually eat alone, because they're embarrassed about how much they eat. This has only recently become recognized as a serious disorder, so the statistics are still few on how many people have it.[10]

Emile Now this anorexia and bulimia thing—it's a "girl thing" mostly, right?

Karen Well, a lot of people think that. Girls and young women do account for about 90 percent of people diagnosed with an eating disorder,

Compulsive overeating or binge eating disorder

a serious chronic eating disorder that involves eating huge quantities of food without purging, feeling completely out of control while doing it, and continuing to eat, even after feeling really full.

but you know, it can affect men too. One of every ten people looking for help with an eating disorder is a teenage boy.

Ryan Yeah. This swim teammate of mine ended up having an eating disorder. He felt a lot of pressure to stay in shape and do well. His dad was diagnosed with cancer and didn't have long to live. They were pretty tight—his dad came to all of our meets—a die-hard fan. So, Nick felt he had to be the best for his dad and bring home that trophy. He thought if he kept his weight down, it would make him faster. But he just got obsessed, and the coach didn't help, either. He was really strict and got pretty nasty if someone gained a few pounds.

Nick was binging and purging for a while before we even found out. One day, during practice, he passed out in the pool and almost drowned. We thought he was pranking us at first. Thankfully, it clicked that something was wrong, and his brother dove in after him.

Emile You mean, no one noticed he was puking in the locker room?

Ryan Nah, he was sneaky. He would take laxatives and diuretics, so we just assumed he had to go a lot.

Like most guys with eating disorders, he was in denial and also pretty ashamed. He didn't want people to think he was a sissy. He thought if he said anything, other people would just rag on him. So, he kept it to himself.

Emile So, laxatives and diuretics—that's how people control the size of their bodies?

Ashley Well, that's two ways, but actually there are many ways to lose weight. That's why it's so easy to get tempted into anorexia or bulimia. Losing weight is addictive.

Diet pills are, like, the most common way, and they're easy to get your hands on. You don't need a prescription. You can get them in a grocery store or drugstore right off the shelf. Same goes for laxatives and diuretics. Seems like everybody carries them in their purses these days. Or you can sneak them from your parents' medicine cabinet.

Emile Well, there has to be some kind of warning on the label of pills, like to talk to your doctor or something, right? I hear that in TV commercials all the time.

Eric Yeah, but teens aren't really all that informed about these things. So, kids might swallow a lot of pills at once, hoping the more they take, the more weight they'll lose. That's pretty scary.

Ashley Yeah, most people don't realize these pills can have serious side effects. And they can start to lose their effect after a few weeks, so you have to take more and more...from what I hear.

Karen All these herbal supplements or teas are supposed to help you lose weight too.

Emile And the kids who make themselves throw up—are all of them sticking their fingers down their throats or what?

Ashley Well, some teens actually use *ipecac syrup,* which is really bad. It's supposed to only be used when you swallow something poisonous or overdose on medicine, because drinking it makes you throw up.

Karen Yeah, and there are those fad diets that never seem to do much but make you hungry and crazy. You know, the low-carb craze, the cabbage diet, the liquid diet, the all-meat diet, the lowfat shakes diet, diet candy bars, and ready-made meals that promise the perfect body. Then there's the good old-fashioned starve-yourself thing. I swear, I can't do that! Even when I have to for a medical test or something, I feel weak and cranky, and all I think about is food!

Jessica Don't forget *liposuction.* Sucks out all the fat right out of your body through a tube, and all you have to do is just lie there.

Eric People use "alternative" ways to lose weight too, like body wraps, appetite patches, hypnotism, fat-reducing creams...

Karen Yeah, like some lotion can make you thinner!

Jessica Actually, I've tried a few. They *don't* work.

Emile Some of the girls I used to hang with would smoke to stay thin. Cigarettes were supposed to kill their appetites, but it didn't work, if you ask me.

Ashley And then there's over-exercising. When you exercise for the right reasons, that's a good thing, but with some people, it gets out of hand.

Jessica Okay, so a few teens weight-watch. There's a difference between worrying about your weight and having an eating disorder. I can't imagine *that* many kids get out of control with their eating.

I've Got This Friend Who...

Ashley Actually, eating disorders are a real big problem. The numbers say 13 percent of high school girls have purged before.[11]

And altogether, about 10 million teens develop eating disorders. Believe it or not, as many as 11 percent of high school students might have one. That means out of every eight people you know, one has an eating disorder, and you might not even know it! Here are some specific numbers:

> Up to 3.7 percent of girls have anorexia.
> Up to 4.2 percent of girls have bulimia.
> Up to 4.2 percent of girls have binge eating disorder.

And lots of times, an eating disorder lasts into adulthood. Like, between 5 million and 16 million people suffer from anorexia and bulimia in the country, and as many as 25 million might have binge eating disorder.[12] Really scary!

Climbing the Scales
Why Someone Might Develop an Eating Disorder

Emile So, why do some kids develop eating disorders?

Karen Well, the reasons fall into three categories: *psychological or emotional, relationship,* and *social pressure* reasons.

Ashley The psychological reasons have to do with low self-esteem, feeling like you're never good enough, problems with how you see yourself, or not appreciating yourself. Maybe you can't figure out who you are or where you fit in. You might think if you look like a certain celebrity or person you look up to, people will like you better.

Eric I also read before that if people are perfectionists, they might have unrealistic expectations of themselves, like being perfect or obsessing about making their body what it's not.

Karen And watch out when you're struggling with stress or problems in your everyday life, even if it has nothing to do with looks or weight. If you aren't careful, you might turn to food for comfort, as a substitute for dealing with the problem. After a while, food can become addictive as a way of avoiding problems. Also, a lot of anorexics feel their life is out of control and think if they keep from eating, at least they have control over *something.*

Eric Also, someone who's depressed, anxious, angry, lonely, or feels empty inside might turn to food as a way to fill the emptiness. But bulimics purge afterward to "undo" their overeating because they don't want to gain the weight. Bulimia is also a way for some kids to express themselves. They might have trouble getting their bad feelings out. So, they purge as a way to express or to "cleanse" themselves, and afterward, they actually feel relieved.

Karen What about relationship reasons?

Ashley Well, with anorexia, kids might get ultra-thin *just* so their friends will accept them or approve of them. Some kids, like, feel actual pressure from other people or even their parents to be a certain way—maybe even to be perfect.

  Like, my mom's *really* big on the thin thing. It's cultural. And my older sister is always looking in the mirror and complaining how "fat" she is. If *she* is fat, then I'm a *cow!* On top of that, my mom's always, like, expected so much from me, my whole life. I have to be the best at everything and look fabulous. She plans everything—my future, my sister's. There's no place for mistakes. Being Porky Pig isn't an option in my family.

Karen A little hard on yourself, aren'cha, Ash? That's a lot of pressure to live with.

Eric I read that if someone has been physically or sexually abused, they are very likely to overeat as a way to bury the trauma, guilt, shame, anger, and pain...and the betrayal. Some kids also think if they get fat, the abuser won't find them "attractive" anymore and will leave them alone.

Karen Or, if kids have a few extra pounds and have been teased about their weight their whole life, they might end up overcompensating and develop anorexia or bulimia as a way to lose weight.

Ryan Okay, let's talk about the social reasons. Obviously, our culture glorifies people who are thin. We're all supposed to have that "perfect" body. Especially if you hang with people who are obsessed with thinness, you could pick up their habits and get sucked into it.

Jessica I can, like, totally relate. I feel pressure to be thin all the time. People constantly judge me on how I look. Do you think I could've gotten to be head cheerleader or homecoming queen if I wasn't a size four? It would be nice if weight didn't matter, but the truth is, it does, especially in certain social groups.

Psychological Factors
❯ Low self-esteem
❯ Lack of self-identity
❯ Feelings of inadequacy or lack of control in life
❯ Problems expressing feelings and emotions
❯ Depression, anxiety, anger, or loneliness
❯ Perfectionism, unrealistic expectations of self

Relationship Factors
❯ Troubled family and personal relationships
❯ Pressure from friends to look a certain way
❯ Overprotective or overdemanding parents
❯ Physical or sexual abuse
❯ History of being teased due to weight

Social Factors
❯ Cultural pressures glorifying thinness and valuing "perfection"
❯ Cultural norms that value physical appearance rather than inner qualities
❯ Association with appearance-obsessed friends or social groups

The Time Bomb *The Chances of Developing an Eating Disorder*

Emile It seems like a lot of the problems that lead to eating disorders affect a whole lot of people. But obviously, not everybody develops an eating disorder. So, who does?

Ashley If someone's, like, already vulnerable to an eating disorder—like if they have a bunch of problems going on, plus they're obsessed with their looks—it can happen.

Karen Yeah. Eating disorders can be sparked when a kid has a shakeup at school or at home—like fighting with a boyfriend, siblings pushing them around, a parent leaving or dying. A transition like puberty, or moving, or starting in a new school, or going away to college can cause an eating disorder too. We're so impressionable at this age, and when we're hurting or feeling lost, it's easy to get influenced. These are the times when we want people to like and accept us more than anything.

Eric There are some specific ages where we're most vulnerable. Believe it or not, the research shows that the ages of nine, thirteen, and sixteen to eighteen are pretty dangerous.

Emile Nine years old? Isn't that way too young?

Eric Not really. Nine years old is usually when puberty hits. Kids' bodies go through such weird changes that everything feels out of whack.

Karen I remember that. I had a friend who went through it earlier than the rest of us. She felt fat because all of a sudden, she had curves in places where the rest of us didn't. She struggled for a while because she didn't like her looks. But we all banded together to support her and always made her feel accepted. At least she didn't feel crazy pressure from us to look a certain way.

Ryan I remember being nine or ten when I started to wonder whether or not my friends and the guys on the sports teams liked me. I had my first crush on this one girl. She was all I could think about, and I wondered all the time if she liked me. I was so awkward back then.

Eric And if there are problems at home—say your parents are fighting—and you start thinking this is what being an adult is like, you might try to "prevent" yourself from growing up and becoming an adult or at least prevent your body from growing up.

Ryan Thirteen is also a dangerous age. All of a sudden, there's a lot more expected of us. It's our first year as teenagers, and we're being initiated into this whole new life. Our parents and teachers expect us to be more responsible and mature. Fitting in and the social scene become a huge thing.

Ashley I'm thirteen, and things are so much different than they were just a year ago. Even my friends expect certain things. They think I can, like, hang out at the mall without my parents, go to certain movies I couldn't see before, and buy certain clothes. There's a whole new set of rules, and the pressure is on.

Jessica So, how are you handling it? You seem so together.

Ashley Ahhh...you really wanna know? Not so good, actually.

Karen What's wrong, Ash?

Ashley I have a confession to make. I don't really know how to say this. It's so hard...

I actually have an eating disorder. I'm anorexic. I've been, like, obsessing about my weight for the last three years, and finally, six months ago, I passed out and ended up in the hospital. Turns out my organs are pretty messed up because I've been putting, like, all this stress on them by not eating and by exercising like crazy. Problem is, when you guys look at me, you see a thin girl, but when I look at me, I see a whale! My counselor says I have a really distorted image of reality, like a fun-house mirror. And it's gonna take a long time for me to see myself like I really am. I've been in therapy for six months and I'm getting better, but I take it one day at a time. It's really tough sometimes. I could fall back into it any time.

Jessica Oh, my god, Ash! Why didn't you say something? No wonder you know so much about this stuff! So, how did it happen?

Ashley Well, let's just say sometimes I feel like I'm in a pressure cooker at home. My parents expect a lot, but my sister never even breaks a sweat. I feel like the loser who can't ever get it right.

Jessica I'm guessing you've talked to your parents about this?

Ashley Yeah, it came out in therapy after we found out I had this problem. We've all been working together real hard to, like, figure things out, to change how we treat each other, but old habits are hard to break. It will take time.

Eric Unfortunately, the vulnerability doesn't end at thirteen. The years from sixteen to eighteen are pretty rough too.

Ashley Oh, great. Something to look forward to.

Eric Well, being older doesn't always mean you can handle everything better. You're doing a great job, so hang in there. But sixteen to eighteen is tough, because that's when we start making serious plans for the future. We're taking intelligence and achievement tests and choosing schools, college majors, and possible careers. Plus, we start to choose our own values and beliefs, separate from our families. So, there's this struggle for control between our way and other people's ways.

Ryan We also start driving at sixteen, so there's even *more* responsibility. And when life gets more hectic, it's easy to feel out of control. So, you look to get some control back any way you can.

Emile Wow! All this stuff reminds me so much of my alcohol addiction—you know, the stuff that led to it and how I felt.

Behind the Looking Glass *Hiding the Evidence*

Emile All right. If eating disorders mess with people's lives, how in the world do they keep it a secret? Seems like it should be pretty obvious to their friends and family.

Ashley Take it from me—people with eating disorders become masters at cover-ups. Anorexics eat almost nothing, but they have their own little "rituals" and get real good at tricking people. They'll, like, take a little food and push it around on their plate to make it look like they've eaten, or cut it up into really small bites and chew each bite thirty-two times. Or they'll pretend to eat but actually spit food out in their napkin. Or get up for a minute and empty their plate in the garbage. Bulimics have little habits that are real tricky too.

Ryan Yeah, I know what you mean. The guy on my swim team was hoarding food in his locker. He'd eat it and then, of course, he'd take a laxative. No one knows you're eating all that food, so no one questions how come you're not gaining weight.

Emile I'll bet binge eaters hoard food too.

Karen Oh, yeah, especially if you have a bunch of people around you who worry about your weight and watch you all the time, you can't have all the food you want in front of them, so you swipe it and hide it for later, when you're alone. So, in front of other people, you just seem like you really aren't eating all that much, and they can't figure out why you're packing pounds. Some binge eaters manage not to gain that much weight, so with them, people have no clue at all.

Jessica And anyone can cover up their weight with clothes, whether you're gaining or losing a lot—at least for a while.

Ashley Obviously, denying or excusing your eating problem is, like, a major thing for people with eating disorders. Anorexics might say they aren't hungry or don't like a particular restaurant.

Ryan Bulimics might say they have a really fast metabolism that makes them go to the bathroom a lot, or they might sneak away without being noticed. If they get caught throwing up, they might say they didn't feel well or overate and "it just came back up." With overexercising, they might say they can't get enough of the sport. Or that the team is counting on them.

How Kids Cope with or Cover Up Eating Disorders

❯ Constantly comparing themselves to others and complaining about weight

❯ Taking a little food and pushing it around on the plate to make it look like they've eaten

❯ Pretending to eat but actually spitting food out in their napkin

❯ Pretending to get up for seconds and emptying the plate in the garbage or back in the food container

❯ Stealing and hoarding food in secret places—the closet, under the bed, their drawers, or the bathroom cabinets

❯ Taking laxatives and diuretics often to get rid of all the "extra" food eaten

❯ Binging alone in secrecy

❯ Sneaking away to eat or purge

❯ Covering up weight gain or loss with loose clothes, certain styles, or certain colors

❯ Constantly coming up with different excuses about why they're going to the bathroom so often or never eating

❯ Denying there's a problem

Eric Binge eaters most likely will deny they're hoarding food, and might just say that being heavy is genetic and isn't their fault. Or they might say they don't know how the food got there. Or throw a tantrum and say you're unfairly starving them.

Ashley And you can hide laxatives and pills pretty much anywhere—in drawers, in pillowcases, under the mattress, in socks, in pockets, in bags of candy.

It's Eating You Up *The Consequences of Eating Disorders*

Emile Having an eating disorder must be a miserable way to live.

Ashley It's not much fun—worrying about how you look all the time or that the way you eat might be killing you. You feel ashamed, guilty, and disgusted. It was so hard for me to, like, have this terrible secret I couldn't fix. Watching my weight, counting calories, exercising, and skipping meals took all my energy. School, hobbies, and family started slipping away. I was, like, an A student all my life, and all of a sudden, I was making Cs! My emotions were all over the place, and I felt totally helpless and really depressed.

Ryan And what really stinks is when people find out, you lose their trust. They never take their eyes off you, are always suspicious, and watch your every move. It's really humiliating, hurtful, and frustrating.

Eric And that's just the psychological consequences. The physical consequences of anorexia and bulimia are worse. It's real hard to get through the day when you don't have the energy to keep going. When you don't eat or you purge, the balance in your body is off. Nutrients aren't going through your body or to the brain so you run out of steam.

Ashley Yeah, the less I ate, the harder it was to keep up in gymnastics or even just participate in class.

Eric Also, anorexics stop eating because they don't think their metabolism is fast enough to burn the calories. But get this: Starving makes their metabolism slow down even more to make up for the lack of food. Ironic!

Ashley Yeah, your heartbeat and your blood pressure slow down too, and that means, like, your blood isn't circulating enough. You get dry skin and constipation, feel cold or dizzy, lose your hair, or even stop having your period. Your heartbeat can get, like, really low. You might pass out like I did.

Karen Bulimia has some of the same side effects, but a few others include sore throat or sores in your mouth and on your gums from all that vomiting. Your *lymph glands* (glands in the neck and other areas of the body that play an important part in your body's defense against infection), which are pretty important to the immune system, can swell too. Blood vessels in your eyes can even burst or you could develop *acid reflux disease*—this horrible condition where acid in the stomach rises up into your *esophagus* (the tube that connects the throat with the stomach).[13]

Also, if you take laxatives, they can cause dehydration, which can make you really sick to your stomach and throw up for real. They can also cause terrible kidney and bladder problems.

Ashley It gets worse the longer you have the disorder. Anorexia can, like, kill your muscle tissue and bone strength. You could develop hair all over your body since it's trying to stay warm. And your sense of reality becomes twisted. You could, like, waste away to nothing. You also might develop gum disease and damage your liver, kidneys, and heart. If you don't get help for the disease, your heart will eventually stop and you will die. Anorexia kills. I think about that every day.

Anorexia Nervosa Side Effects	
Short-Term Side Effects	**Long-Term Side Effects**
❯ Feeling weak ❯ Constantly being cold ❯ Feeling dizzy ❯ Trouble concentrating/focusing ❯ Lack of motivation or hyperactivity ❯ Dry skin ❯ Constipation ❯ Losing hair ❯ Weak pulse and low blood pressure ❯ Metabolism slowing	❯ Total focus on weight and food intake ❯ Reality badly distorted (hearing "things" or seeing yourself as fat when you're very thin) ❯ Hair developing all over body to keep it warm ❯ Loss of bone strength ❯ Lack of nail growth and strength ❯ Extreme weight loss ❯ Gum disease ❯ Losing your period ❯ Losing muscle tissue (body "eats" it when starving) ❯ Damage to heart, liver, kidneys, etc. = DEATH

Bulimia Nervosa Side Effects	
Short-Term Side Effects	**Long-Term Side Effects**
❯ Trouble concentrating/focusing ❯ Swelling in lymph glands in neck ❯ Sore throat ❯ Acid reflux ❯ Sores in mouth and on gums ❯ Blood vessels in eyes bursting ❯ Low blood sugar and blood pressure	❯ Loss of tooth enamel from stomach acid contact ❯ Acid reflux disease ❯ Dependence on diuretics and laxatives (body muscles "forget" how to function) ❯ Severe addiction to binging and vomiting ❯ Ruptured esophagus ❯ Ipecac syrup storing in heart muscle and destroying it = DEATH ❯ Damage to heart, liver, kidneys, etc. = DEATH

Eric Bulimics can lose their *tooth enamel* (the hard covering over the teeth), because their stomach acid is in contact with their teeth, causing their teeth to break easily. Their esophagus might rupture because of all the throwing up. Or they could become dependent on diuretics or laxatives, since their body muscles "forget" how to work. Diuretics can cause kidney and heart damage too. And ipecac syrup—if you use it a lot, it builds up in your heart muscle and breaks it down. Then, you're a goner!

Obesity
being extremely
overweight

Karen On the flip side, binge eating brings bad stuff to your life too. What's scary is it can lead to *obesity*—another word for being extremely overweight. It's ironic—we're so obsessed with weight, but we're the fattest nation in the world, and getting fatter every day. Obesity is the number one health problem among kids in the country. Two of every three adults are overweight—that's like 100 million adults. And something like 16 percent of kids and teenagers are overweight or obese![14]

That's more than 12 million kids—three times the number of kids who were overweight or obese twenty years ago. Extra body fat weighs you down both physically and emotionally. Most overweight kids who are binge eaters grow up to be overweight or obese adults. They become the "yo-yo dieters," struggling with their weight and dealing with a poor body image their whole lives. They've been teased and picked on plenty, and that can cause them to have really bad self-images and never go after their dreams.

Plus, binge eaters may be eating all that food to suppress an even bigger problem in their life no one knows about. So, they're much more likely than other people to develop mental problems, become severely depressed, or even kill themselves. And feeling like you have no control over your eating can be horrible for your self-esteem, happiness, and ability to get by or build healthy relationships with other people. You're so ashamed of what you're doing, and you don't want anybody to see you like that.

Eric But the physical problems of binge eating and obesity are even worse. Binge eaters are more likely to have liver, heart, and pancreas damage. Obesity is a big risk factor for a bunch of health problems, like diabetes, high blood pressure, high cholesterol, heart disease, sleep problems, infertility, and even cancer.

Until recently, these problems happened mostly to overweight adults. Now, all of a sudden, they're happening to kids! More than 100,000 people die every year in the United States because of obesity.[15]

Ashley The worst part is, without treatment, like, up to 20 percent of people with eating disorders will die.[16] Scary.

Binge Eating Side Effects	
Short-Term Side Effects	*Long-Term Side Effects*
› Weight gain › Joint stress and disease › Masking a much deeper problem that needs to be seen so the person can get help › Feeling out of control, disgusted with yourself, anxious, or depressed	› Becoming overweight or obese › Weight fluctuations for years › Potential heart, pancreas, or liver damage › Health problems like diabetes, high blood pressure, infertility, or cancer › Joint stress and disease with possible replacement of joints › Continuing to live with a much deeper problem that goes unnoticed and does not get dealt with for years › Developing major anxiety, depression, or other severe mental health problems › Never going after the things in life you want

Mirror, Mirror, on the Wall
Warning Signs of an Eating Disorder

Karen So, how can we tell if someone we care about suffers from an eating disorder?

Ashley Well, there are a bunch of signs for anorexia, so pay attention.

Could You or Your Friend Have Anorexia?
- Are you so terrified of the idea of becoming fat that all you do is think about it, compare yourself with others, and diet?
- Have you gotten thinner but continue to diet—even losing 15 percent or more of your ideal body weight?
- Do you think you're fat even though everybody else tells you you're extremely skinny?
- Do you continue dieting or denying yourself food when everybody else is really concerned about you?
- Do you deny you are hungry when you're starving?
- Do you cut up food into really small bites, push it around on the plate, and chew each bite many times?
- Do you obsess about food, nutrition, and cooking (reading serving guides, recipes, and cooking for others a lot) but avoid eating?
- Do you feel guilty or ashamed after eating?
- Are you losing your hair or is strange hair growing all over your body?
- Are you dizzy a lot or have you lost consciousness from starving?
- Are you often tired or out of energy, barely able to focus and get anything done?
- Are you cold even when the temperature is fine?
- Has your period become irregular or stopped?
- Do you wear baggy clothes to hide how thin you are, so people won't worry?

Karen For bulimics, some warning signs are the same. But bulimia is usually harder to pick up on, because bulimics aren't always skinny. Here are some additional signs.

Could You or Your Friend Have Bulimia? Additional Warning Signs
- Do you compare yourself to other people all the time, not feeling you're as thin as them?
- Do you complain about being "bloated" or "sick" almost every time you eat?
- Are you disgusted or guilty about your body and the way you look?
- Are you obsessive about overexercising?
- Do you weigh yourself all the time?
- Do you purchase large quantities of food and eat them very quickly?

- Do you steal or hoard food everywhere, like in your closet, drawers, medicine cabinet, car, locker, or gym bag?
- Do you binge often when you are alone?
- Do you run to the bathroom all the time and after every meal to purge what you ate?
- Does your weight bounce up and down frequently?
- Do you feel guilty or ashamed about eating?
- Do you have an overwhelming feeling of being out of control and use food as a way to control something in your life?
- Has your period become irregular?

Ryan The warning signals for binge eating include all the signs for bulimia except for the purging, plus these:

Could You or Your Friend Have Binge Eating Disorder? Additional Warning Signs
- Have you gained a lot of weight quickly and keep gaining more and more?
- Are you unable to eat in moderation and lose any weight?
- Has your weight gone up and down your whole life?
- Do you eat large quantities of food when you feel bad or have a problem you don't want to deal with?
- Do you often need to eat a lot to feel better?
- Do you continue to eat even after you feel extremely full?
- Do you lie to other people about how much you eat?

Lifting the Lid Off the Pressure Cooker
Breaking the Cycle of Eating Disorders

Ashley You know how they say the hardest part is admitting there's a problem? They weren't kidding. For me, the hardest thing ever was to accept I had a problem that I couldn't control. Sometimes things happen and you get in trouble. And then, you have to find a way to, like, get out of trouble before it costs you your life. I couldn't make it better on my own.

Jessica So, what does a kid do if that happens?

Ashley Well, I got really sick. I passed out and ended up in the hospital. Scared my parents to death. I knew I needed help. I broke down and told them. It wasn't easy, but at least I didn't have to go through it alone or suffer in secret anymore. This huge weight, like, came off my shoulders.

Then we talked about everything, and I told them how I felt I didn't live up to their expectations. My parents had to learn to, like, back off, and believe me, that was hard. And I had to learn I would never be perfect and accept that. Well, every day is a struggle, but I'm getting better and I'm gonna beat this.

Emile You go, Ash! That's the spirit! What else would you recommend to kids struggling with an eating disorder?

Ashley Stay away from people who push you to an eating disorder, even if it's not on purpose. If you hang around people who are, like, obsessed with weight and constantly talk about being fat or dieting, or purge, or stuff themselves, or whatever, you're gonna be in danger of getting sucked back in. You have to keep the temptation and those people away. It can be really hard if they're your friends, and even harder when they're your family.

My mom and my sister had to be, like, much more sensitive, and they did try. But if you have friends who don't, you have to walk away.

Eric What else?

Ashley Well, it really helps to get support from your friends. Our society is obsessed with thinness, so it's everywhere—on TV, in music videos, in magazines. When you feel, like, weak or tempted, you need other strong, caring people to be with you, to hold your hand, talk to you, sit on that couch with you after you eat, or even watch you or stop you from purging, whatever, to help you stay strong, and get through the hour or the day.

Your parents are especially important. They can cook the food for you, watch you eat everything on your plate, and then keep you from running to the bathroom to puke. It's a partnership: They're there for you, and you do your part. You try your best and speak up if you feel

---

What to Do If You've Reached the Boiling Point

> *Admit to yourself there's a problem you can't fix alone.*

> *Confess to an adult you trust* and know will do everything possible to help you. Your parents, another relative, a guidance counselor, a school nurse, a favorite teacher or coach, a minister, or a friend of the family are good choices.

> *Stay away from people who tempt or push you* toward an eating disorder with everything they say and do about weight and food.

> *Tell your friends and ask them to be sensitive to your problem and support you* through it with words and deeds.

> *Commit to getting professional help* and stick with it until you really *are* better.

out of control. On top of that, knowing someone, like, has your back gives you the strength to face the bad times.

Karen And if it's your friend who has an eating disorder and asks for help, don't get freaked or push her away. Listen and be there for her!

Jessica What if you think something is wrong with a friend, but she hasn't, like, said anything?

Ashley Well, I'd be really honest but still sensitive. You could say you're concerned about the fact that they've lost a lot of weight and ask if they're feeling okay.

Ryan It's important not to judge and to stay neutral. And don't tell your friends to "just stop"—obviously, they can't. Ask lots of questions so you can understand better. And the one thing you *should* tell your friends is to absolutely tell an adult—someone they trust!

Jessica Like they're going to do that! What if they just say "no" or say they will and then don't?

Karen Then you have to do what's right and tell an adult yourself —their parents or your parents are your best first choice.

Jessica If I did that to a friend, she'd be so mad at me, she'd never talk to me again!

Eric Yeah, it could happen, but I think one day, she'd understand you were just trying to help and forgive you. And besides, consider the alternative.

Handy tip

If you suspect someone you care about might have an eating disorder, tell a parent, teacher, counselor, or another adult you trust. You won't be tattling. You'll be saving a friend's life!

Turning Up the Heat: Bringing Up the Sensitive Subject When You're Worried about a Friend

➤ "I notice you've lost a lot of weight, and I am concerned. Is everything okay?"

➤ "I saw this movie about this girl who was denying herself food or always on liquid diets, just like you. She had a serious eating problem that was very dangerous. Is there something you wanna talk to me about?"

➤ "You've been avoiding me lately—I miss you. What's going on?"

➤ "I'm sorry to hear about your problem. Please let me help you get through it. What can I do?"

I've Got This Friend Who...

Food for Thought *Avoiding Eating Disorders,*
Saving Friends from the Slippery Slope, Spreading Awareness

Emile Getting help when you already have an eating disorder is one thing. But how do you guard against it in the first place?

Ashley Watch out for two big things. The first is how you feel about yourself, and the second is dealing with other problems that could, like, drive you to look for comfort and control in food.

Karen You're totally right. Self-esteem has such a huge impact on a person's weight. Obsessing about the whole image thing can become a pretty nasty cycle. If the people who are important to you make you feel you don't measure up—whether they're your family, friends, or people you look up to, like the popular kids or even your favorite celebrities—you will start judging yourself through their eyes, and pretty soon, you'll feel the same way about yourself.

Eric Also, teens don't always think about the natural changes our bodies are going through. A lot of stuff happens that we can't control! Sometimes, it's a growth spurt—getting a lot taller—and you gain the right amount of weight. Sometimes, you could gain the weight and *then* get taller. You know?

Jessica Well, with all the pressures from everybody *on top of,* like, the stuff Mother Nature throws our way, it's hard to not be hard on ourselves. So, how can we stop it?

Emile It sounds cheesy, but I think what makes sense is for you to talk to an adult if you're really unhappy with how you look. Parents, aunts and uncles, nurses, school counselors, or teachers can always offer support. Plus, they've been there and get it.

Jessica I never would have even *imagined* telling one of my teachers or a counselor something that personal!

Ryan Hey, a lot of our teachers and counselors are cooler than you think! I've turned to some of them when I needed someone to talk to, and it helped a lot. You need allies—everybody does.

Eric The point is, if you feel loved, emotionally supported, and unconditionally accepted, there's a better chance you'll avoid getting into trouble.

Jessica Well, yeah, but you also have to, like, eat right and stay fit. I love junk food as much as the next person, but I know if I have too many chips or burgers, I'm gonna gain weight.

Karen Yeah, that is important. And a lot of kids don't know much about nutrition or how to eat right. So, it's important we get educated. When you know how much of what your body needs, it helps you pay attention to the ingredients in different food products, and not only calories but also nutritional content like *protein, carbohydrates,* and *fat*. That helps you make smart choices.

Eric Exercise is important too. You shouldn't go nuts, but running, swimming, Rollerblading, or anything that gets your heart pumping for at least half an hour every other day is really good for you and does help keep your weight down. So, if you do that, it's less likely you'll look for other, more dangerous ways to slim down.

And it's also important to be around people who like you the way you are and appreciate everything about you—not just your looks. And friends who boost your ego by telling you when you look good, so you don't feel desperate to starve or stuff yourself. People who say nice things—about your clothes, your hair, but also your sense of humor, your math abilities, or whatever—and who raise your self-esteem are the ones you should hang with.

Ashley Yeah, if your friends make you feel like the "chubby one" or the least attractive one, you'll be tempted to do whatever it takes to be "worthy" to run with that crowd. I used to feel that way with my sister.

Jessica Let's get one thing straight, Ash. You're a beautiful girl. And I don't say that often.

Three Main Nutrients We Get from Food and Use as Energy Sources
Protein A large molecule composed of one or more chains of amino acids that's required for the structure, function, and regulation of the body's cells, tissues, and organs. Proteins are essential components of muscles, skin, bones, and the body as a whole. Proteins provide four calories of energy per gram.
Carbohydrates Mainly sugars and starches that can also be defined chemically as neutral compounds of carbon, hydrogen, and oxygen. The body breaks down most sugars and starches into *glucose*, a simple sugar it uses to feed its cells. Carbohydrates produce four calories of energy per gram.
Fat A compound formed from chemicals called fatty acids, also used as an energy source by the body. Fats are high in calories, providing nine calories of energy per gram.[17]

I've Got This Friend Who...

Amounts You Need from Each Food Group Every Day[18]

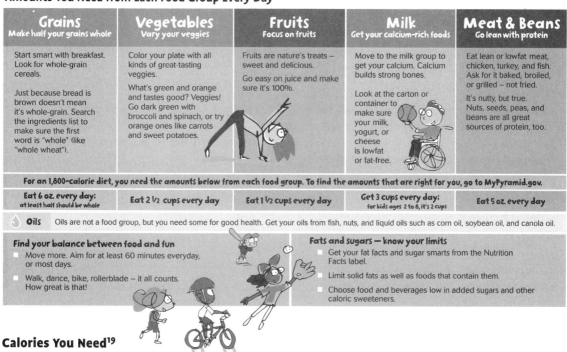

Grains Make half your grains whole	**Vegetables** Vary your veggies	**Fruits** Focus on fruits	**Milk** Get your calcium-rich foods	**Meat & Beans** Go lean with protein
Start smart with breakfast. Look for whole-grain cereals. Just because bread is brown doesn't mean it's whole-grain. Search the ingredients list to make sure the first word is "whole" (like "whole wheat").	Color your plate with all kinds of great-tasting veggies. What's green and orange and tastes good? Veggies! Go dark green with broccoli and spinach, or try orange ones like carrots and sweet potatoes.	Fruits are nature's treats — sweet and delicious. Go easy on juice and make sure it's 100%.	Move to the milk group to get your calcium. Calcium builds strong bones. Look at the carton or container to make sure your milk, yogurt, or cheese is lowfat or fat-free.	Eat lean or lowfat meat, chicken, turkey, and fish. Ask for it baked, broiled, or grilled – not fried. It's nutty, but true. Nuts, seeds, peas, and beans are all great sources of protein, too.

For an 1,800-calorie diet, you need the amounts below from each food group. To find the amounts that are right for you, go to MyPyramid.gov.

Eat 6 oz. every day; at least half should be whole	**Eat 2 ½ cups every day**	**Eat 1 ½ cups every day**	**Get 3 cups every day;** for kids ages 2 to 8, it's 2 cups	**Eat 5 oz. every day**

Oils Oils are not a food group, but you need some for good health. Get your oils from fish, nuts, and liquid oils such as corn oil, soybean oil, and canola oil.

Find your balance between food and fun
- Move more. Aim for at least 60 minutes everyday, or most days.
- Walk, dance, bike, rollerblade – it all counts. How great is that!

Fats and sugars — know your limits
- Get your fat facts and sugar smarts from the Nutrition Facts label.
- Limit solid fats as well as foods that contain them.
- Choose food and beverages low in added sugars and other caloric sweeteners.

Calories You Need[19]

1,800–2,400 calories daily Teen girls (fourteen to eighteen years old), depending on how physically active you are. More activity requires more calories.

2,200–3,200 calories daily Teen boys (fourteen to eighteen years old), depending on how physically active you are. More activity requires more calories.

If you don't belong in these age groups, you can find your calorie requirements at www.mypyramid.gov.

Ashley Thanks!

Emile Well, if you think any of your friends don't feel good about their looks, the same advice goes for them. They might be embarrassed to say anything. But if you know someone really well, you get that gut feeling something's off. You can usually tell when they're acting weird or something's bothering them. So, take them out for a salad and use that as an excuse to bring up the issue of food.

Karen Just like you need reassurance, your friends do too. So, you need to let your friends know you like them for who they are—not just their looks.

You should also be there for friends if they're having troubles in their lives. Be a friend and partner with the whole weight thing too, and work together to help them be healthy and happy with their looks. And encourage them to let adults in too.

Balancing the Food Equation: What to Do for a Friend Whose Body Image Is in the Dumpster

> *Compliment the things you like about her* as often as you can. Knowing your friends like you and are proud to be seen with you is a huge ego booster. Your compliments will influence your friend to see herself in a positive light too.

> *Let her know you don't always feel fantastic about your body either, and share some of the things you struggle with,* so she realizes no one's body image or life is perfect. Everyone has days when they feel unattractive, face challenges in their lives, or just want to hide from the world. It helps her understand it's okay for her to not be perfect.

> *Assure her that healthy, happy, beautiful people come in all shapes and sizes* and that being really skinny is not the only way to be beautiful. She needs to learn to be comfortable in her own skin and like all the good things about herself instead of always beating herself up for the "bad" ones.

> *Advise her to face and work out problems in her life before they get out of hand,* and not to turn to food for comfort. Offer your support and make it known that you'll be there for her.

> *Encourage her to find activities and hobbies to help her define who she is and how she feels about herself*—whether it's sports, the student government, drama, painting, or volunteering—instead of relying only on her looks. This will help people notice her for her personality and accomplishments—not only her physical appearance.

> *Suggest you both learn how to eat better and exercise enough.* Make a pact to work together and look out for each other. Get more information on nutrition. Pick a physical activity you both like—whether it's running, biking, or swimming—and do it three to four times a week. Balance is everything, and teamwork often gets the job done when going solo doesn't.

> *Recommend that she keep a journal with her thoughts, feelings, and activities related to weight, food, and eating.* This makes it easier to keep track and determine how serious the problem is—both for her and also for any adults or professionals who might need to jump in later if things get worse.

> *Gently suggest that she talk to an adult about her worries about weight and her body* and offer to go with her when she does. Sometimes, perspective and advice from someone older and more experienced—whether it's your mom or the school nurse—can make all the difference.

Jessica Okay, so a friend comes to me and says, "I'm fat; I need to go on a diet," when the truth is she's already skinny! What should I say?

Eric Well, let's brainstorm some things you can say.

Food for the Soul: Things You Can Tell a Friend Who's Unhappy with His or Her Looks

"That's a great sweater. Red looks really awesome on you!"

"Thinner is not always the same as prettier or healthier."

"It's important to eat when you're hungry and stop when you're full."

"There's no 'perfect' body—people come in all shapes and sizes. So, you don't need to look like anybody else. You have your own look, and you're attractive just the way you are."

"Hey, I feel 'blah' sometimes too. Everybody does now and then. I'm sure you're being much harder on yourself than anyone else. Give yourself a break."

"If you really don't like the way you look, talk to me about what is bothering you, and we can figure it out. Exercise, makeup, and the right outfit can make a big difference too."

"Food is not your enemy. Let's find some nutrition information and figure out how much of what foods we need every day."

"If you are sad, mad, or bored, find something fun to do other than eating."

"Try out different hobbies or activities, like drawing, sports, or theater, to see what you're good at. It will make you feel good about yourself, and it's a great stress reliever. It will also help people see you as more than just a pretty face and body. Isn't that what you want—to be liked for who you are, not just what you look like? I know I do."

"You know what—I've been kinda down on myself about those five pounds I gained too. Let's go talk to Nurse Jenkins—I know I sure could use some advice."

Where to Get Help

Emile So, where does a kid look for help if he already has a problem with food or feels like he's slipping?

Ashley Well, like we said before, the first place to look for help is with a caring adult who's gonna take you seriously and want to help you. Home's the first choice—but if you don't feel like you'll get much understanding there, turn to a guidance counselor, teacher, minister, or even your family doctor. They're all trained to deal with people's problems.

Karen Your next choice is the phone book or Internet. Just look up "eating disorders" in your local Yellow Pages or go to the Yellow Pages online at http://yp.yahoo.com, choose your city, and type in "eating disorders." Local clinics and treatment places are listed there that you can call to get information and help.

Ashley There are also a bunch of great organizations and Web sites.

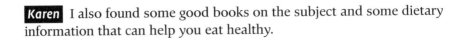

Karen I also found some good books on the subject and some dietary information that can help you eat healthy.

Web Sites

National Eating Disorders Association
www.nationaleatingdisorders.org
This Web site carries detailed information on all the eating disorders and where to find help if you're in trouble. The association also has a toll-free information and referral helpline: 1-800-931-2237.

National Institute of Mental Health
www.nimh.nih.gov/publicat/eatingdisorders.cfm
This Web site provides valuable information and resources to help you understand, cope with, and beat an eating disorder.

American Psychiatric Association
http://healthyminds.org/multimedia/eatingdisorders.pdf
This online brochure entitled "Let's Talk Facts about Eating Disorders" gives thorough information about the causes and effects of eating disorders, as well as additional resources.

TeenCentral.Net
www.TeenCentral.Net
The home page of this award-winning teen Web site by the children's charity KidsPeace links to a specific weight awareness section that helps, supports, and guides older kids and teens to face and work through weight issues, problems, or crises such as eating disorders, providing valuable information that can save your life.

My Pyramid Food Guidelines, U.S. Department of Agriculture
www.mypyramid.gov
The U.S. Department of Agriculture's nutrition policy and promotional Web site provides daily recommended calories and servings from each food group, dietary guidelines, and tons of other nutrition information to help you eat right and balance your weight for life.

Books

The Luckiest Girl in the World by Steven Levenkron

The Best Little Girl in the World by Steven Levenkron

Running on Empty: A Novel about Eating Disorders for Teenage Girls by Anna Paterson

So Now You Know: The Battle of a Teenage Girl Fighting Her Eating Disorder in Silence by Darah Echevarria

Preventing Eating Disorders among Pre-Teen Girls: A Step-by-Step Guide by Beverly Neu Menassa

Fit to Die: Men and Eating Disorders by Anna Paterson

Additional Resources

Web Sites

My Pyramid Food Guidelines, U.S. Department of Agriculture
www.mypyramid.gov/downloads/miniposter.pdf

**Dietary Guidelines for Americans, 2005,
U.S. Department of Health and Human Services**
www.health.gov/dietaryguidelines/dga2005/document/

Books

All Made Up: A Girl's Guide to Seeing Through Celebrity Hype and Celebrating Real Beauty by Audrey Brashich

The Thinnest Girl Alive: Diary of a Young Dancer by Alissa Hall

The Eating Disorder Solution by Dr. Barbara Cole

Eating Disorders by Ra Bryant-Waugh

Eating Disorders by Trudi Strain Trueit

Eating Disorders and Obesity: A Comprehensive Handbook (2nd edition) by Christopher G. Fairburn and Kelly D. Brownell

Males with Eating Disorders by A. Andersen

Body Talk: The Straight Facts on Fitness, Nutrition, and Feeling Great about Yourself! by Ann Douglas, Julie Douglas, and Claudia Davila

Food Fight by Kelly Brownell and Katherine Battle Horgen

Women Who Hurt Themselves by Dusty Miller

Chew on This: Everything You Don't Want to Know about Fast Food by Eric Schlosser and Charles Wilson

Fast Food Nation by Eric Schlosser

Self-injurious behavior (SIB): What is it? It's hurting yourself on purpose. The most common way kids hurt themselves is by cutting their arms, legs, or other areas of their body with a sharp object. But there are other ways that are less visible and sometimes preferable, because they don't leave scars or visible marks others can question. Kids who engage in SIB are usually really determined to keep it a secret. But the statistics that do exist—which are incomplete at best—are hinting that the problem is much bigger than any of us might think.

What would drive a child to hurt himself or herself like that? Well, it seems self-injury is a drastic form of expression when kids aren't able to say the words out loud or when they think no one will listen or understand. It can also be a punishment for some traumatic event in kids' lives that they think is their fault, or a distraction from their emotional pangs that refocuses their attention on the physical pain self-injury causes. It could also be a way of turning anger on themselves when they need an outlet and know that hurting other people is not acceptable.

—*Peter Langman, Ph.D.*

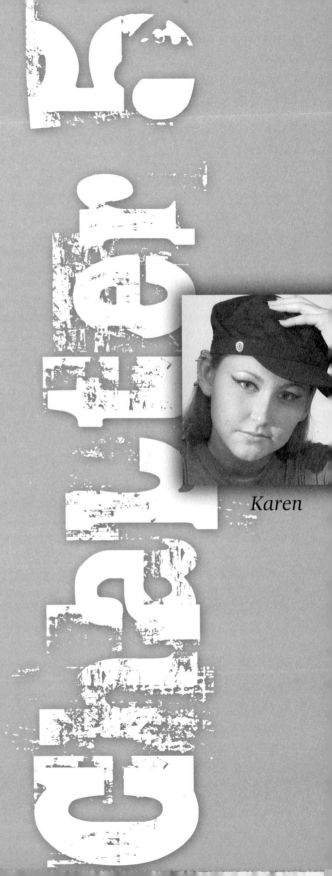

Karen

Regardless of the reasons, SIB seems to help kids feel better, and this is why—just like other destructive behaviors like drinking or doing drugs—it can become addictive. Kids might need to do it every time they feel bad, and it might even become a reflex. It may be a temporary fix, but it is important to understand that SIB is not a solution to the problems you may be struggling with. It is dangerous—both physically and mentally.

The good news is you don't have to live with SIB and suffer in silence. There are ways to stop, and you can get help to learn how to deal with stresses and problems in your life in more positive ways that heal your body and mind instead of harming them. Helping friends who might be self-injuring is also extremely important—even though you might be frightened or put off by what your friend is doing. Your friendship and support can give that person the strength and motivation to get help and cut SIB out of his life. You can change and even save your friend's life.

—*Mary Ann Swiatek, Ph.D.*

CUTTING YOURSELF DOWN

The Painful Truth about Self-Injurious Behavior and How to Heal the Scars

Jessica   Eric   Ryan   Emile   Ashley

Scarred *The Facts about Self-Injury*

Jessica I met this girl at a party the other night. She seemed so cool, and we really hit it off. At one point, we were in the bathroom fixing our makeup, and she rolled up her sleeves to wash her hands. Oh, my god, you guys won't believe what I saw! She had all these scars on her wrists and up both her arms, like she had tried to kill herself, you know? And there were a bunch of them, like she did it several times! I felt, like, so uncomfortable that I just made some lame excuse and ran out. Then I avoided her for the rest of the night. I felt like such a bad person, but I just didn't know what to do. I was so freaked!

Eric Well, from what you described, it sounds more like *SIB* than suicide attempts.

Jessica SIB? What's that?

Self-injurious behavior (SIB)
deliberately hurting yourself and causing physical damage to your body for the purpose of emotional relief

Eric It stands for *self-injurious behavior*—deliberately hurting yourself and causing physical damage to your body to gain emotional relief. So, these people hurt themselves on purpose. It's a harmful behavior people can't stop, an addiction even—sometimes a lot like alcohol and drugs. Many of them *need* to self-injure to get through the day, and they can't stop. Sadly, people of all ages really do suffer from SIB, and it's nothing to poke fun at or take lightly. Although it may sound totally crazy, it is a very real problem for many kids and teens, and it is much more common than you think. The statistics aren't certain, but it's estimated that at least two to three million Americans over twelve years old self-injure.

Ashley I have heard of it. Some girls at the place where I was getting counseling for my eating disorder were being treated for cutting themselves. That's what people with SIB do, right—cut?

Indirect damage
damage to the body and a person's health over time from activities such as smoking cigarettes, drinking alcohol, or doing drugs

Ryan Well, cutting is the classic example. But a lot of things fall in the self-injury category. The self-injury can be *direct* or *indirect,* with the same result—it causes harm and damage to the person's body.

Indirect damage, like alcohol, tobacco, or drugs, takes its toll on you after a time, causing some serious physical problems and illnesses like heart, lung, kidney, liver, and brain damage; diseases; mild or serious injuries; or even death. But that's damage that sometimes takes years to get.

Direct damage causes pain and harm to the body immediately after it's done.

Direct damage
damage to the body and a person's health causing pain and harm to the body immediately after it's done, creating health dangers that can be very serious, even deadly

Since we've already talked about alcohol, tobacco, and drugs, let's focus on the *direct* types of SIB today.

Jessica Okay, so what are they?

Eric Let's break down ways you can do direct damage to your body. First, *cutting*—the most common self-injurious behavior. Arms are the most commonly cut area, but the wounds can be made anywhere on your body. Some people make just random cuts, and other people carve symbols, words, or images.

Ryan Then there's *rubbing* or *scraping*. Also, *banging* or *punching*—basically like beating yourself up. Next comes *biting*. And *picking* is another one, which is basically constantly picking at wounds or cuts you already have, preventing them from healing.

Karen I know about *pulling out hair*. I had this friend in middle school who would pick a hair on her head and then just yank it out. Then, a couple of minutes later, she would do the same thing again.

I've Got This Friend Who...

Emile Well, the ones I know about are *inserting objects into the body* and *ingesting things* you're not supposed to.

Jessica Sounds like this episode of *Ripley's Believe It or Not* I saw on TV once where people were putting these, like, round wooden chips inside their ear lobes or lower lip—so their lobes and lip were like the size of an egg! Or this guy who was putting this string up his nose and, like, pulling out the other end from his mouth! Or another guy who had all these, like, hundreds of pins stuck into his skin all over his body. So, are these people, like, self-injuring?

Karen Maybe, but more likely, they're just weird! I'm kidding. But, the difference is, some people do it for cultural reasons, the novelty, or because they want to have a "trick" nobody else has. And others do

Types of Direct SIB
› **Cutting** Using a sharp object such as a knife, razor blade, scissors, broken glass, sharp piece of metal, or any other sharp object to deliberately scratch or cut the skin
› **Rubbing or scraping** Rubbing or scraping a rough object such as a nail file, fingernails, an eraser, or another harsh object on your skin to the point that you start to bleed
› **Banging or punching** Inflicting harm to the body by punching the fists, or banging the arms, legs, or head against a floor, wall, pole, or other hard surface to cause pain and damage, as well as hitting parts of the body with a hard object like a brick, metal pipe, hammer, or bat
› **Biting** Intentionally using your teeth to bite or chew on fingers, arms, lips, or other areas of the body, breaking and tearing up your skin
› **Picking** Continually picking at wounds, scratches, or scabs to cause pain, prevent the healing process, and make existing injuries grow more severe
› **Pulling out hair** Ripping and tearing large quantities of hair off your head or body, or pulling out eyelashes or eyebrow hairs
› **Inserting objects into the body** Piercing different parts of the body with pins or other sharp objects and inserting the items—sometimes permanently—under the skin or fingernails or inserting items into openings in the body
› **Ingesting things** Swallowing items that aren't meant to be eaten—like coins, paper clips, nails, or pieces of glass
› **Burning** Putting lit cigarettes, matches, lighters, hairstyling irons, or other sources of heat against the skin on purpose to cause painful burns[1]

it because they physically and emotionally need to—that's when it's a serious problem.

The last type of direct self-injury is *burning*, which is self-explanatory.

Eric A lot of kids suffer from this awful, self-destructive condition. And the sad thing is, most of the time, even when it's happening to kids around us, we might not know it for months or years. It's a behavior that's very well covered up. Most people who self-injure do it in secret, so it's hard for people around them to know. So, because of that, no national statistics exist on SIB.

On top of that, different researchers define SIB differently. Some researchers define it as any behavior that can cause harm to the body, both *indirect* and *direct*. Other researchers don't include *indirect damage* in their definition. That leads to a wide range of results among studies, because the criteria they use to determine how often it happens are not the same.

Falling Short—SIB Stats (and Their Shortcomings)
> Unlike a behavior such as suicide, there are no national statistics on self-injury.
> Studies that have been done on SIB tend to be very limited in scope and do not reflect the true extent of the problem.[2]
> Research studies on the number of adolescents who engage in SIB report rates ranging from 4 percent to as high as 38 percent.[3]
> At least two to three million Americans over the age of twelve self-injure.
> One study of 440 teens from urban and suburban high schools found that 13.9 percent reported engaging in some form of SIB. Of that 13.9 percent, 64 percent were girls and 36 percent were boys.[4]

Walking on Broken Glass *What Drives Kids to SIB?*

Jessica I don't understand why any kid would do something like that.

Ryan Well, it's hard to know exactly what problems get kids to the point where they choose to hurt themselves. But cutting and other forms of SIB are signals the person suffers from significant emotional pain. Just about anything traumatic or painful can set it off: depression or anxiety about something going on at home, loss, death, problems with a boyfriend or girlfriend, trouble with friends, rejection, struggles at school, or combinations of things.

I also heard that if a kid has suffered through some kind of major personal trauma—like physical or sexual abuse—SIB might become their relief. Abuse can set off some pretty intense feelings like guilt, anxiety, self-hate, depression, helplessness, and anger, and all that stuff can cause people to turn to self-injury to cope—just like they might turn to alcohol or drugs.

Eric Yeah, they're obviously suffering from serious problems, and they feel like they can't ease their pain any other way. These are kids who feel isolated and full of pain. Their desperate need to find a way to release their pain drives them to do terrible things to their own bodies.

Jessica Yeah, okay, but with alcohol, drugs, or even risky things that give you a rush, at least they're fun. Why do SIB instead of other, like, more enjoyable methods for escaping pain or stress? Why would you want to scar up your body like that?

Ryan Well, some people just have a really hard time handling intense emotions. I mean, we all do, but for some people, it's just completely unbearable. So, when they can't deal anymore, they turn to SIB as a distraction. They feel like when they cause themselves physical pain— because it's destructive and it *does* hurt—it draws their attention away from the emotional pain, forcing them to focus on the physical pain for that moment. Obviously, it works, or people wouldn't be doing it. Just think about it—if you accidentally cut your finger or you fall and bruise your knee, your whole attention goes to the pain there—and you're not thinking about anything else at that moment, right?

Eric Another reason some people do SIB is as an outlet for their bottled-up pain, frustration, confusion, sadness, or anger—to let it out some way, because it's too much to keep inside. Some people aren't able to use words to express their feelings—like talking to other people or writing it in a journal. They might not be very good with words or might feel the other person just won't understand. So, they resort to hurting themselves instead as a way to express all the negative emotions that are weighing heavy on them. SIB is like a silent message—even a silent scream to release the negative energy.

Karen Even when people can express their feelings, they might have had negative experiences sharing them with other people who betrayed their trust and made them scared to do it again. If you talked to a friend about a personal problem and they told other people or freaked out on you, chances are you won't come to them again.

On top of that, in some families, a kid's feelings never seem to matter. Kids are made fun of or ignored when their feelings are hurt. They're told to just "get over it" or "deal with it." So, when they feel intense emotions, they might turn them on themselves, to get rid of them somehow without attracting unwanted attention.

Ryan Other kids who self-injure say no words could ever really express the pain they are in. To show their level of distress, they feel they have to do something more drastic than just talking. Hurting themselves sends a *much more* powerful message about their emotional distress to anybody who's paying attention—especially if they *want* to get caught. If they're doing it and don't bother to cover up the scars, it's a cry for help, and they're hoping somebody *will* notice.

Eric Others feel like whatever it is they're dealing with is so terrible and unspeakable that they just *can't* tell anyone. They feel like it's a deep, dark secret no one could ever find out. But the feelings they have are really strong, and they still need to deal with them somehow. That happens with people who've been sexually abused. They often feel it was their fault or they were responsible somehow and blame themselves. They might start believing they're really bad people and need to be punished. So, they self-injure to punish themselves.

Ryan Or they might do it for the opposite reason—to regain a sense of control that was taken from them when the other person betrayed their trust and violated them. They figure by "taking matters into their own hands," they're getting some control back. I've heard girls who were date-raped might start doing SIB for that reason.

Karen Other kids say they do it because they feel numb inside—from whatever they might have gone through—and they want to make sure they can still feel something—*anything.* They resort to drastic ways to "wake themselves up."

Emile And other people might hurt themselves to stop themselves from hurting other people. If you're really angry at somebody for what they've done or just really bitter and angry in general, but you know it's not socially acceptable to take it out on other people, you might turn the violence on yourself. At least that's something nobody has to know about. I just thought about that because this girl Aisha I used to know had all this anger and resentment at the world—not that I blame her, 'cause she'd been through more stuff that you can even imagine. But she would do things to herself all the time. She would do more and more piercings on herself and play with razor blades, putting them in her mouth and stuff. She'd cut herself up or stick needles into her arms and legs. I would ask her why, and she would just smirk and say, "Beats blowing things up."

Eric Some kids injure themselves to copy others. If kids see somebody they look up to do it—especially if they're going through something and get the message it's helping that other person feel better—they might try it to see if it will work for them. Sometimes, kids will just try it to fit in with a new group that might be doing it and pressuring them to do it, especially with stuff like piercings or tattoos. Kids already doing it will make it seem "cool."

Karen I've also heard that, as a last resort, some kids might do it as an alternative to killing themselves, which is a social taboo and forbidden by some religions. If you're in so much pain that it's unbearable, but killing yourself is not an option, you might try self-injury instead. It's less drastic and less permanent, but it might relieve some of your distress for a while.

Ryan Yeah, good point, Karen. People think self-injury is automatically a sign a person wants to kill themselves, and that is not always true. Self-injury and suicide are different conditions, usually caused by different states of mind. People who self-injure usually don't want to die—they want to find a way to deal with the distress so they can avoid killing themselves. On the other hand, people who are suicidal usually have given up and don't believe there's any other way they can deal with their pain.

Because the self-harm helps people in major emotional distress reduce the pain, it might actually lessen the risk of suicide. But even though SIB and suicidal behaviors are different conditions, it is important to

Why Might Kids Self-Injure?
❯ To deal with negative feelings that are overwhelming
❯ To relieve the bad feelings internally instead of telling someone, which might be seen as weak
❯ To relieve the pain of a deep, dark secret in a way that will keep others from discovering it
❯ To be distracted from psychological/emotional pain
❯ To feel "numb" when in too much distress
❯ To "feel something" instead of feeling numb or empty
❯ To reduce or express anger or rage
❯ To communicate the real extent of the emotional distress to other people
❯ To self-punish for "messing up" or "being bad"
❯ To prevent hurting other people, which is not socially acceptable
❯ To copy others who self-injure
❯ To relieve painful feelings without committing suicide

	Self-injury	Suicide
Purpose	› Relieve pain › Find a temporary solution	› Escape pain › Find a final solution
Pattern	› Often behavior is repeated over and over › Often different methods are used at different times	› Few repetitions › Usually only one method is attempted
Type of emotional pain	› Comes and goes › Very uncomfortable, but not completely intolerable with some coping techniques	› Constant › Completely unbearable, even with coping techniques
Outlook	› Some periods of optimism	› Hopelessness and helplessness all the time
Outcome	› Temporary improvement of emotional state after self-injury	› No improvement in emotional state if suicide attempt is not successful › Death if attempt is successful[5]

remember that people who engage in SIB could become suicidal at some point if SIB is not relieving the pain well enough. If they face some big crisis all of a sudden, they could become overwhelmed to the point of suicide. Also, some people go back and forth between being self-injurious and suicidal, depending on how desperate they feel at that moment.

Desperate Measures *When Does SIB Usually Start?*

Eric Most kids who turn to SIB start in seventh or eighth grade. Of course, that's when puberty begins. Kids entering adolescence face not only the changes to their bodies, but also issues about their identity, relationships, dating, and sexuality for the first time. It's a time that brings much greater stress, and it can be overwhelming. Also, we start to spend more time away from our families and become more independent. So, when stressful situations come up, we might feel more reluctant to go to our parents because we don't want them to think we can't handle things on our own. If the stress becomes too much, SIB might be a way to deal.

Emile Boy, I remember how out of control things started to feel when I was in middle school. Everything seemed to be changing real fast. I didn't have anyone to talk to at home, but that's always been the case. My dad hasn't been around in years. My stepdad was a monster. And my mom has always worked several jobs and has had to deal with my younger brothers and sisters. I met Aisha when I was twelve. At that time, I actually thought it was kind of cool. I thought she had to be pretty tough to do that stuff without even blinking. And being tough is everything in the neighborhood I came from.

Eric Other kids are also vulnerable to SIB, including kids already dealing with other mental or emotional issues or in mental hospitals. Also girls with eating disorders—like you, Ash. They're unsatisfied with their body image, and when they get really angry with themselves for never "getting it right," they might punish themselves. Other kids who are vulnerable are those who've been sexually abused, like we said before.

Ryan Yeah. Changes during adolescence create sexual feelings that are normal. But for people with a history of sexual abuse, these feelings might remind them of the abuse and bring up all these traumatic memories and the pain they felt. For them, the whole sexuality thing can raise really disturbing issues. They also feel guilty that they're having these feelings that, in their mind, have to do with this bad thing. So, they might feel angry and disgusted with themselves. At the same time, when other people are interested in them, they fear being taken advantage of again. So, all this intense stuff from all these new feelings can make them start hurting themselves.

Heartbreak *The Risks and Dangers of SIB*

Karen Well, SIB sure isn't a healthy way to cope with stress, and it obviously creates a lot of risks and health problems. There's always the chance people will hurt themselves more than they planned. Like cutting deeper than they intended or swallowing something that turns out to be more harmful than they expected and really messes with their insides. You could cut or injure some veins or major organs, and if you're swallowing random things, you could scar your throat, or your intestines. You could puncture your stomach or god knows what else. You could end up having your stomach pumped or an operation to remove whatever you swallowed. With self-injury, kids run the risk of permanently damaging themselves—physically, mentally, or both. The worst of it is you could end up killing yourself even though you weren't trying.

Eric Also, there are the scars, wounds, or burns. You get trapped in this place where you're constantly ashamed of your body and want to cover it up as much as you can. That's gonna affect your self-esteem and the way you feel about your body for sure—and carry over into your relationships with other people too.

SIB Side Effects	
Short-Term Side Effects	**Long-Term Side Effects**
❯ Risk of injury or even death ❯ Temporary scars ❯ Shame and guilt ❯ Social isolation ❯ Avoiding dealing with the issues and feelings causing the SIB in the first place ❯ Injuries that require medical attention but go untreated	❯ Disability due to severe injury ❯ Permanent scars ❯ Constant shame and low self-esteem ❯ Difficulties with relationships ❯ Depression or other mental problems ❯ Danger of starting up again after you've stopped when things get crazy in your life ❯ Avoiding getting help for the issues and feelings that are causing SIB in the first place ❯ Physical damage to the body that goes untreated and might lead to severe injuries or death

Plus, scars attract attention and uncomfortable questions from other people, so you feel constantly under pressure to hide them. Then some people see them, realize what they are from, and don't want to get involved. They run, like Jess did. You might just withdraw little by little from other people completely to avoid the questions and judgment. After a while, it could lead to severe depression or anxiety. So, it's not over when you stop SIB.

Ashley And you must feel so out of control doing this thing to yourself—and, like, *needing* to do it.

Ryan Not to mention, kids who self-injure are suffering mentally and emotionally, and the issues never get resolved, so they could get worse over time.

Keeping It to Yourself
Living with SIB and Keeping It in the Closet

Eric Well, considering the lack of statistics on SIB, it's pretty obvious that most kids are so ashamed of it that they will do whatever it takes to keep it a secret from family, friends, everybody.

Karen Plus, coming out with SIB would also raise questions about why they're doing it in the first place—where the pain is coming from and what exactly SIB is helping them deal with. That opens up a whole other can of worms they might not be ready for, so they have a double reason to keep it under wraps.

Ryan And what makes SIB even trickier is that the person could be acting normally on the outside. SIB gives people relief from their problems—at least temporarily—so they can go back to being "normal" after they do it. So, in front of you, they might seem like the most fun-loving people, which covers up the problem.

Karen Obvious cover-up techniques are to cut or burn in places that people don't normally see. They might do it on their stomachs, their chests, the inside of their thighs, or even around their private parts. Or throw on a long-sleeved shirt, oversized sweater, or long pants.

Eric In a warmer climate, it might be harder to hide it. Some girls wear lots of bracelets or makeup over the cuts. If kids are cutting their stomachs or chests, they avoid bikini bathing suits or taking their shirts off.

Ryan Kids who do SIB try to compensate for it in every other way, so nobody has even the slightest hint.

Emile And people who do show it off—they've made it out to be this really trendy thing that's all about image—being cutting-edge. Like something that adds to their self-expression and personality. Because that's become mainstream fashion in some forms these days—like ear piercing, belly button rings, tongue rings, nose piercings, tattoos—most of us don't really give those a second thought.

Karen When people realize they need help and are desperate to stop, they might give it away and somehow let other people know. They might casually roll up their sleeves—like that girl at the party—or wear clothes that might reveal a small part of it so others will be tempted to ask. Or as a last resort, they might just tell you and act like it's no big deal, but

---

Living with the Terrible Secret: How Kids Hide SIB

➤ Not confiding in anyone

➤ Cutting in places not normally visible

➤ Wearing clothing that covers their arms and legs

➤ Not wearing two-piece bathing suits, or not taking their shirts off

➤ Flaunting SIB in socially acceptable forms like tattoos and body piercings in "cool" places

➤ Doing SIB in ways that make people think it's part of their image and self-expression

that's rare. Usually, it's much more likely they'll show you before they come out and say the words. I don't blame them—they're most likely afraid you won't know what SIB is exactly and will get scared, turned off, or just plain freak. I mean, it must be very difficult to just drop it in casual conversation, like, "Let's catch a movie later. Oh, by the way, I cut myself when I'm unhappy."

The Scars...Literally *The Warning Signs of Self-Injury*

Jessica So, you're telling me there's almost no way to tell if one of my friends or even my sister self-injures?

Karen I'm saying it's pretty hard to tell...but it's not impossible. Scars on the body—particularly the arms—are obviously the main warning sign. Cuts, scrapes, wounds, scabs, burns, carved figures—they most likely signal SIB. But always keep in mind that the scars may have been caused by something else the person is just not comfortable talking about. If you've known the person for a while—if she's a really good friend or your sister—and the scars were never there before, that would be a pretty good hint SIB is going on. The point is to pay attention.

Ryan Yeah, so if the person always wears long-sleeved shirts and refuses to wear T-shirts in gym class or a bathing suit at the pool, you should keep that in mind, plus anything unusual you might see by accident. People who keep themselves well covered all year long might have

SIB Signs and Symptoms
❯ Having scars, bruises, broken bones, or wounds that don't ever seem to heal, or burn or bite marks
❯ Always wearing long pants and long sleeves, even in hot weather
❯ Refusing to wear a bathing suit
❯ Not telling you how the scars got there when you see some
❯ Giving you explanations that don't add up or make sense
❯ Getting irritated, worked up, or leaving when you bring up the issue
❯ Flaunting new tattoos, piercings, or other body "enhancements" all the time
❯ Doing piercings and body "modifications" personally, frequently without going to a professional

other reasons to cover up, like not liking their body or having childhood scars, so it's no guarantee of SIB, but there's a chance it could be.

Eric And if you do see some scars by accident, or if the person exposes them openly but won't tell you how she got them or gets worked up when you ask, those are also signs. So are bogus excuses that don't match the scars—like if she has several cuts on the inside of her arm and says her hand slipped while she was cutting something.

Ryan Pay attention if your friend seems to be popping up with a new tattoo or body piercing every day and can't seem to stop doing stuff like that to his body, especially if he's doing it himself instead of going to a professional.

Healing the Wounds *Getting Help for Your SIB or Helping a Friend Stop Hurting Themselves*

Karen The bottom line is, SIB happens to good people. It might even happen to you. You don't have to just live with it and let it take over your life, or leave your friend to struggle with it alone.

Ryan Right on. If you're hurting yourself, there are some things you should know. First, you need to understand that it is normal to have bad days or bad feelings. Everyone has them sometimes. Sometimes, life just gets out of hand and even becomes unbearable. But, you can learn safe, healthy ways to handle your distress and let others know without resorting to drastic measures. You need to try to figure out what makes you feel like hurting yourself. Is it too much pressure at school, anger toward your parents, arguments with friends, not being accepted, being teased or bullied, memories of bad things that happened to you, traumatic things you've had to face recently like losing someone close to you, or an unexpected change in your life that's making you very emotional or scared?

Karen Second, I think you have to remember that just like drinking or doing drugs, hurting yourself doesn't solve the problems. All you get is temporary relief at a high price.

Third, write down the problems you're dealing with and next to them, list *all* the possible solutions you can think of besides SIB. Every problem has several solutions—it may not feel like that when you're hurting, but give yourself the time to think about it. Once you have your list, try the positive things to see if they *do* make a difference and make you feel better. If they do, you might discover you don't need to self-injure to feel better.

Seven Steps to Beating SIB

1. Remember that bad feelings are normal, and everybody has trouble in life sometimes—you're not alone.

2. Remember that SIB provides temporary relief at best and doesn't really solve any of your problems.

3. When the urge hits, distract yourself by doing something else for ten minutes, then ten more, and ten more, until the urge is less strong.

4. Try to identify the things that make you feel like hurting yourself—the problems you're dealing with and the bad feelings they're causing.

5. Think about each problem and write down *all* the things besides SIB that might be solutions you could try.

6. Find a caring, trustworthy adult to confide in and ask for help.

7. Get professional help from a counselor or therapist to work through your feelings and find healthy, positive alternatives to SIB when the going gets tough.

Eric A bunch of positive solutions help problems we've already talked about, including talking to a friend or a sibling whom you can trust not to blab to the whole world. If you don't think you have a friend like that, then get some new friends. But also, find a dependable adult you can share your issues with—especially the fact that you're hurting yourself—and ask for help. Anyone you feel close to and comfortable with—anyone who makes you feel safe and cared for—from a special teacher to the guidance counselor, a family friend, the parent of a friend, an aunt or uncle, a minister, or even a neighbor you're close to. Of course, your parents are a given, but we sometimes feel like our parents have way too much invested in us and would just flip out. Then again, some kids are very close to their parents. Whatever your case is, go to an adult. Grown-ups know more stuff than we do, and if they have your best interests in mind, they will try to help you deal with whatever problems you face. Just don't give up.

Ryan Sometimes, it's hard to stop self-injuring by yourself, even if you have your friends' or your parents' support. So, a counselor or therapist can help you learn healthy ways of expressing your feelings, and how to identify and solve problems before you reach the breaking point. With the right help, you can learn positive ways to deal with emotional scars that are causing the physical scars.[6]

Ashley What if you find out a friend is hurting herself to deal with problems in her life? It's such a sensitive issue. How do you, like, go about helping her?

I've Got This Friend Who...

Eric Do your best not to react negatively to the person. Treating somebody like a freak doesn't encourage open conversation and self-confidence.

Karen True. People need to be able to share something like that with you and know you're not gonna abandon them when they need you most. They already feel isolated and ashamed of what they're doing. So, stay calm and listen to them with concern and sympathy. Avoid saying anything that will make them feel like they're stupid or crazy. Let them say what's going on without feeling like they've upset you or lost your friendship. Ask questions—like how they feel, why exactly they self-injure, and what SIB does for them—how do they feel after injuring themselves?

Ryan Then do with them what you would do for yourself. Sit them down and talk about a bunch of other possible solutions they can try besides hurting themselves to deal with whatever problem they're facing. They could range from talking to their parents if they feel like they aren't getting enough attention, to finding more fulfilling activities that make them feel like winners if they're feeling like losers, to getting help and treatment if they're suffering from a poor body image or an eating disorder.

Eric Then, you should advise them to talk to an adult they feel comfortable with or ask for professional help. You can offer to go with them or talk to somebody on their behalf. You could even tell them the two of you can call a helpline without giving your names and just talk to a professional about what your options are.

If a Friend Is Self-Injuring...	
Do's	**Don'ts**
❯ Stay calm. ❯ Be respectful. ❯ Be caring and don't make a fuss. ❯ Ask your friend questions to understand where the SIB is coming from. ❯ Encourage your friend to get help from an appropriate adult. ❯ Offer to go with your friend to the adult or talk to someone for him.	❯ Don't try to handle the problem yourself or keep it a secret. ❯ Don't talk about suicide if the person does not identify the behavior as suicidal. ❯ Don't use "put-down" language like "stupid," "crazy," or "sick." ❯ Don't act afraid, shocked, or disgusted. ❯ Don't avoid or reject the person. ❯ Don't make fun of the person or make light of the situation.

Ashley But how do you bring it up to a friend who you think is hurting herself, but she doesn't actually tell you? What if she, like, gets really angry at you for asking?

Eric Remember, people who self-injure are already upset and feel like they are at the end of their rope. You have to ask yourself if keeping a friend safe or even saving her life is worth the chance she might be mad at you.

Emile You know, this whole "how do I talk to friends and say that I'm worried about them without making them angry" thing just keeps coming up with everything we've talked about so far. The bottom line is, no pain, no gain. You might as well accept it and learn that a little discomfort, awkwardness, and even hurt feelings will be part of it. It's worth paying that price ten times over if it means you can help your friends live better lives or even save their lives. No, it won't be fun, but yes, you *should* do it anyway. Isn't that what friendship is about?

I think just to make it as painless as possible for both of you, you should bring it up very casually, without making it into a "thing," but you also shouldn't joke or make light of it. You could say something like, "Hey, I saw your arm the other day. It reminded me of this friend I had in middle school who was having all this trouble and was cutting herself to help deal. Are you doing that? If you are, I won't think any less of you. But maybe I can help you, and we can work through whatever's bothering you." Something like that is nonthreatening. You're not making your friend feel like a freak, but you are letting the person know you've noticed, you understand, and you're there.

And if you don't make any headway with getting your friend to go for help, then you *gotta* tell somebody. There is a huge difference between snitching and getting help for people who are at risk for seriously hurting themselves. You can't just sit by and watch them end up in the hospital or, even worse, in a body bag.

Ashley No, you're right. And how can we prevent people from self-injuring in the first place?

Lock Up the Razor Blade
Preventing SIB from Tearing Up Your Life

Eric Several things can help you prevent SIB, just like they can help you prevent almost any other bad decision or action. The first one is to build good relationships with several key people in your life and have a good, strong, solid support network—a group of both other kids and adults that you can trust with your life and can go to with anything. Not only family and friends, but also teachers, school counselors, family friends, or even religious leaders in your community. As an adolescent, being able to talk about your concerns, questions, and feelings with other people is really important and having someone to go to will help you fight the urge to do unhealthy or dangerous things.

The second thing you need to do is find healthy outlets for your emotions. Like, there are thousands of ways to deal with stress besides SIB. Many of these outlets—like activities you enjoy that make you feel happy or good about yourself—give you the chance to meet new people, improve your mind, strengthen your body, express yourself, and let your creativity shine...and have an awesome time too. Stress is a fact of life, but it doesn't have to cause you to hurt yourself and put your health in danger.

Handy tip
Find positive activities that help you relieve stress, rather than self-injuring.

Karen True. Some examples of positive activities that help you relieve stress are sports, playing an instrument, listening to good music, exercising, doing yoga and meditation, making time to relax and think about things, keeping a journal, writing stories or poetry, doing volunteer work, joining a community youth group or choir, painting, drawing, doing crafts, or joining a faith-based group or a club at school (like drama or science). Anything that gives you a chance to put your talents and energies into positive things will make you feel better about your life, and your problems won't seem quite as overwhelming.

Eric The third thing you need to do is learn to respect and value your body. You know that whole "your body's a temple" thing. Take that to heart. You only have one body, and it needs to last the rest of your life. And you're gonna be around for a long time, so you have to treat your body well and take care of it. This means telling yourself that doing things to hurt yourself is not allowed or acceptable—tell yourself that every day, until you believe it for real.

Here's the last thing: You have to learn to stand up for yourself. If you can't protect your rights and set boundaries, plenty of people in your life will take advantage of you, exploit you, push you around, or abuse you. Being able to find ways to express your likes or dislikes, maintain your beliefs and values in the face of peer pressure, and make it known when other people are crossing the line and not treating you right is a major part of becoming a strong, confident adult.

Karen Yeah, so if you have a problem with how another kid behaves with you, how your parents treat you, how your friends pressure you, or anything else other people are doing that you dislike, you need to learn to express yourself and stand your ground. That doesn't mean being rude, a nag, an abuser, or a snitch. But it *does* mean letting people know what's okay and what's not okay.

➤ Establish good relationships and a strong, solid support network that includes peers and trustworthy adults you can turn to in times of need.

➤ Find healthy ways of handling your emotions, such as:
   ➤ Participating in sports, whether on a formal team or just for fun
   ➤ Learning to play a musical instrument
   ➤ Listening to good music
   ➤ Spending time with friends
   ➤ Practicing yoga or meditation
   ➤ Making time to relax
   ➤ Keeping a journal
   ➤ Writing stories or poetry
   ➤ Painting, drawing, sculpting, or doing crafts
   ➤ Volunteering in the community
   ➤ Joining a community youth group (such as SADD or a choir)
   ➤ Joining a faith-based group (such as Bible study) or a school club (such as drama or math)

➤ Treat your body with respect and kindness.

➤ Learn to stand up for yourself, your values, and your decisions.

Where to Get Help

Ryan If you're dealing with this terrible secret—SIB—log on to TeenCentral.Net. We've talked about it before, and it's a great, safe place to share your troubles with other kids your age and find support from peers around the world. Just reading some stories might make you feel less alone in what you're going through. You will get clinically screened advice from professionals too.

Emile And this great Web site by the Nemours Foundation also has really good, solid information on anything and everything relating to physical and mental health, the problems in our lives, and more. It has a page for kids and a separate page for teens.

Karen The American Self-Harm Information Clearinghouse has tons of articles on SIB too. And the SIARI (Self-Injury and Related Issues) Web site is an international resource with all kinds of information and other links. If you're in trouble with SIB, you should check that out too.

Web Sites

TeenCentral.Net
www.TeenCentral.Net
This free, anonymous teen Web site by the children's charity KidsPeace gives you a safe place to share your problems with peers and trained counselors who can help you find healthy alternatives to SIB when problems become hard to handle.

KidsHealth.org
www.kidshealth.org/teen
This teen Web site by the Nemours Foundation offers several pages on SIB, its causes, effects, talking to friends about it, and how to end the cycle.

American Self-Injury Information Clearinghouse
www.selfinjury.org
This Web site has many SIB articles and related information to help you understand SIB better.

Focus Adolescent Services
www.focusas.com/SelfInjury.html
This Web site is a clearinghouse of information and resources on teen issues to help and support you and your family through problems, including self-injury.

Self-Injury and Related Issues (SIARI)
www.siari.co.uk
This Web site offers international links and resources to help you find answers, inspiration, and support if you suffer with SIB.

S.A.F.E. (Self-Abuse Finally Ends) Alternatives®
www.selfinjury.com
The Web site of this nationally recognized treatment and education network offers information and resources that can help you stop hurting yourself.

Hotline

1-800-DONT-CUT (1-800-366-8288)
You can call this hotline from anywhere in the country if you need help or need to know more about SIB right away.

Additional Resources

Web Sites

American Academy of Child and Adolescent Psychiatry, "Self-Injury in Adolescents," Facts for Families
www.aacap.org/page.ww?name=Self-Injury+In+Adolescents&section=Facts+for+Families

The Mayo Clinic, "Self-Injury/Cutting," Mental Health
www.mayoclinic.com/health/self-injury/DS00775

American Association for Marriage and Family Therapy, "Adolescent Self Harm"
www.aamft.org/families/consumer_updates/adolescent_self_harm.asp

The Palo Alto Medical Foundation, "Self-Injury and Self-Mutilation"
www.pamf.org/teen/life/suicide/selfinjury.html

ACT for Youth Upstate Center of Excellence, "Self-Injury Fact Sheet," Research Facts and Findings
www.actforyouth.net/documents/facts_aug04.pdf

athealth.com, "Self-Harm"
www.athealth.com/consumer/disorders/selfharm.html

Books

Healing the Hurt Within: Understand Self-Injury and Self-Harm, and Heal the Emotional Wounds by Jan Sutton

The Scarred Soul: Understanding and Ending Self-Inflicted Violence by Tracy Alderman

Slice at Life by Jolynn Tumolo

In Harm's Way by Emily Caballero

I've Got This Friend Who...

Eric

Taking risks has its rewards, especially when the risk is tied to something you really want that can truly make your life better and more meaningful. We all take risks to a greater or lesser extent, whether it's in our relationships, our professions, or our life choices. Some risks are worth taking—those from which you might gain a lot, while the cost if you lose is small.

However, some risks are not worth taking—those that put you or somebody else in considerable danger without bringing any benefit to your life. These kinds of risky behaviors include using drugs, stealing, running away, reckless driving, having unprotected sex, or even taking part in risky sports. Unfortunately, these are the types of risks kids and teens are most likely to take, when risk-taking can seem like a cool way to be independent or escape problems. Teens might be more concerned with looking cool than long-term issues like future health or happiness. Experimenting is definitely part of growing up, but when it leads you down a path that brings you harm, the price is too high. The key is to know your boundaries. Something that will hurt you physically or emotionally, take away your promise of a bright future, harm someone else, or even end your life isn't worth the excitement or praise of your friends.

—David E. Woodward, L.C.S.W., C.A.C.

HIGH-RISK BEHAVIOR

A Roller-Coaster Ride to Disaster

Jessica   Ryan   Karen   Emile   Ashley

High-Risk Behavior *What's That?*

High-risk behavior
doing risky or
dangerous things that
can cause trouble or
damage, or may hurt or
kill you or someone else

Eric Okay, our next topic is *high-risk behavior*. That's basically doing risky or dangerous things that can get you into trouble, get you or someone else hurt, ruin your future, or even kill you. Some kids are called "high risk"—they do risky things on a regular basis and seem like they need to do them to feel good about themselves.

Karen What qualifies as high-risk behavior?

Eric Well, obviously, drinking, driving drunk, smoking, doing drugs, having eating disorders, hurting yourself on purpose, or even attempting suicide—all that stuff's high-risk behavior. But we've already talked about those. What we haven't talked about is all the other risky things kids do—whether accidentally or on purpose. Things like driving recklessly, shoplifting, stealing, vandalizing, acting out, getting into fights, breaking and entering, gambling...

Karen There are other things too: running away, joining gangs, body piercing, tattooing, having unprotected sex, putting yourself in dangerous situations, and even doing high-risk adventure sports.

Ryan Many high-risk behaviors go hand in hand, so kids end up doing more than one at a time. Like drinking and then driving drunk in a stolen car. You have three high-risk behaviors there that put you in even more danger than if it was only one thing.

Ashley So, like drinking and then going to the house of a stranger and having unprotected sex? That's three risky things. Right?

Ryan Yep. And the more risky stuff you do, the more likely something bad will happen.

But some kids do it anyway. And they pay the price—sometimes a really high one, like my brother did. I read that in 2002, more than 5,000 teenagers sixteen to nineteen years old died in car crashes. More than 15 percent of all car accidents involve teens, and they're four times more likely to have a car accident than older drivers.

On top of that, the risk for having an accident doubles with the number of teen passengers. So, if there's one teen passenger, the risk goes up two times, and if there is a second teen, the risk goes up four times.

Eric Well, here's what I found that's even scarier: The U.S. Centers for Disease Control and Prevention do a *Youth Risk Behavior Surveillance* survey every two years. The most recent one, from 2005, says 71 percent of kids who die between the ages of ten and twenty-four die from car accidents, injuries, murders, and suicides.[1]

Know what else I found? A lot of kids really do risk it all. Check out these stats.

Startling facts

Seventy-one percent of kids who die between ages ten and twenty-four die from
> Car crashes
> Unintended injuries
> Homicide
> Suicide

According to a 2005 survey,[2] many high school students reported the following:

1. Doing a number of things (in the past twelve months) that increased their risk of unwanted pregnancies or sexually transmitted diseases (STDs), including HIV:
   > 46.8 percent engaged in at least one sexual encounter.
   > 37.2 percent did not use a condom during sex.
   > 2.1 percent admitted to injecting an illegal drug at least once.

2. Doing a number of things that increased their risk of getting hurt or sick:
   > 23.0 percent smoked cigarettes during the past thirty days.
   > 13.1 percent were overweight.

3. Doing a number of things (in the past thirty days) that increased their risk of dying:

- 43.3 percent drank alcohol.
- 9.9 percent drove a car or other vehicle after drinking alcohol.
- 28.5 percent rode with a driver who had been drinking alcohol.
- 10.2 percent hardly ever or never wore a seat belt.
- 83.4 percent hardly ever or never wore a bicycle helmet.
- 20.2 percent used marijuana.
- 3.4 percent used cocaine.
- 35.9 percent got into physical fights.
- 18.5 percent carried a weapon.
- 8.4 percent tried to kill themselves.

Ryan Anyone could do risky stuff and have bad judgment once. No one's perfect. The thing is, most of us might do it because we don't realize what we're getting ourselves into, or it's curiosity, a onetime thing. And once we understand how dangerous it is, we back off. But some people do it on purpose and don't back off even when it catches up with them.

The difference is basically doing something risky once in a while—that's called *use*—and doing it all the time and continuing to do it, even if it hurts and you know it's gonna end badly—that's called *abuse*.

Emile Right. So, it's basically the difference between being curious and being in trouble. We're all curious. But most people, when they feel a bad effect—like they lose money, lose friends, trash their car, get sick, feel out of control, have pain or get hurt, or feel guilty—they'll quit doing it. Now, if a person keeps doing it even though bad things happen, that means they can't help it. It's another way of saying the person is addicted.

Addiction is basically when you're so dependent on something that you have to have it, and it doesn't matter what price you pay. You're willing to put up with anything just to not be without it. And the more you do it, the more used to it you get. You build *tolerance*—it doesn't affect you the same way as before. So, to get the same feeling, you have to up the dose or the risk every time. Just like with drugs. It works the same way for all risky behaviors when you're addicted.

On top of that, if you stop doing it, you suffer symptoms of *withdrawal*. You can feel dizzy, sick to your stomach, nervous, irritated, angry, or really scared for no reason. You could sweat, feel cold, feel hot, have problems sleeping at night or eating. You could feel totally out of control. You have this really strong craving accompanied by really unpleasant feelings and need more of the stuff. So, you have to have it again to stop the craving.

When you're addicted to something, it's really tough to stop, whatever the behavior is. It might be cutting yourself, taking drugs, shoplifting, overeating, fighting, gambling, or chasing other dangerous thrills. But continuing to do it just makes you more and more addicted. Vicious cycle.

Jumping Off a Cliff *Why Do Kids Put It All on the Line?*

Jessica Well, peer pressure is definitely one reason some kids do risky things—because they're pushed by their friends. They want to fit in, or everyone else seems to be doing it. They think it's normal, and they'll be left out if they don't. But peer pressure can't be the only reason.

Ashley Yeah, like what about the kids leading the pack and forcing others to act in high-risk ways? Or the kid who does high-risk behaviors alone? Peer pressure obviously doesn't explain that.

Ryan Good point. After my brother died in the drunk-driving accident, I was so angry with him for doing that to himself and to us. None of it made any sense. He had everything going for him—why would he just risk it all for something so not worth it? My mom's a psychologist, so we talked about why he was drinking and getting high, and why he was joyriding in a stolen car with a driver who was high.

Peer pressure is definitely not the only reason. Another reason is that risky things can seem fun and give you a real high. Driving fast gives you a rush—you feel like you're flying and it's a blast. Same with adventure sports. Challenging yourself is exhilarating—it gets your blood pumping. Well, same goes for doing something you aren't supposed to—and getting away with it. And when it's "wrong" or "forbidden," it's that much more exciting.

Another reason is if you're the kind who gets bored quickly and you're looking for something new and interesting. If it's something you've never done before, you're curious and it's too tempting to pass up.

Karen Or you're so desperate to be liked that you're willing to do anything. Say you're poor and people at school are always putting you down for your dinky clothes. Then you go to the mall and see this awesome sweater, but it's so expensive that there's no way you could ever afford it. You think to yourself, "Maybe I can swipe it without getting caught," and you go for it. And you actually get away with it! Wow, what a rush— I mean, you feel so totally exhilarated and in control of things. And on top of that, you now have this great sweater. That little voice in the back of your head that says it's wrong—you just blow it off.

Eric And also, when you feel alone or like you don't fit in with anyone, you think doing something risky with other people will bring you closer because you're sharing this secret. So you're part of something "special." Or things are so bad and you're so down and depressed that you want to just take your mind off your problems and feel better—any way you can. Or you're so numb inside that you wanna feel something—*anything*. We've already talked about alcohol and drugs being a huge temptation when your emotions are all over the place. It's the same with other risky things.

Emile Here's another reason: You want to show everybody what a big shot you are—how much faster, stronger, braver, smarter, better you are. You want to be in charge and have people admire you and follow you. So, you do something that nobody else dares to do—like cheat on that test with the teacher from hell or jack that Mercedes convertible in broad daylight.

A lot of kids also do stupid stuff—like getting into fights, shoplifting, vandalizing, having unprotected sex, or whatever—just to get attention. They feel like everybody's ignoring them, so they do something drastic to stand out.

Eric Other kids are just fed up with rules. They have had it with people telling them what to do. They want to feel independent and in charge of their lives.

Another reason is a family history of doing high-risk things. Maybe your dad, mom, or older brother drinks, smokes, uses drugs, steals, runs

Why Do Kids Do Risky Things?

❯ In response to peer pressure

❯ To reduce boredom and try something new and exciting

❯ To feel less alone or belong to something

❯ To change other people's image of you

❯ To escape feelings of depression or pain

❯ To assert yourself as a leader and earn others' respect and following

❯ To get attention

❯ To show you're independent and you'll do what you want

❯ Because other family members are doing it, you look up to them, and want to be like them

High-Risk Behavior

in a gang, gambles, or is into binge eating. You just follow in their footsteps. You do what you're taught. Makes sense—right?

Karen All these high-risk behaviors share a common thing. Kids get a rush from doing them. This feeling of *euphoria* makes kids feel they are on top of the world, in control, and even invincible. We all love that feeling—like when you nail a test or are the first to cross that finish line. We've all felt that way, and it's totally great! Right?

Eric Yeah. The way it works is when your body thinks you're in danger, it produces a chemical called *adrenaline*. Then your brain sends it all over the body to reduce pain and discomfort. That gives you that natural high. That's what's so fun about roller coasters—they fool your body into thinking you're in danger, and you get that adrenaline rush.

Problem is, that feeling only lasts for a little while and then, boom—it's gone. Now, usually, with things like setting a record, you get it naturally. And it's so cool, people wanna feel that way again. So, a lot of people get into competitive sports so they can. But some people don't want to work that hard—they just want the rush fast and easy. And they might try to force it to happen by taking risks.

Karen Risky stuff is sometimes so thrilling. It's an easy way to make you feel you're in control and everything is awesome. The rush is immediate. So, chances are you'll end up not discriminating between things that only imitate danger and things that are actually dangerous. Pretty much anything goes, as long as you get the rush, so you could end up really gambling with your life.

Eric Then before you know it, you get addicted to that feeling, and you become an "adrenaline junkie."

Ryan Or, if you do something risky by accident, or because someone pressures you, but you end up liking the way it felt, you will most likely do it again. So, you could become addicted to the thing that gives you the feeling too.

Jessica So, you could get addicted to the feeling and do risky things to get it, or you could get addicted to the risky thing because it gives you the feeling?

Ryan Yup—or both, which is worse. You get a double whammy. For instance, if you like how you feel when you drink, you can get addicted to the feeling. Plus, you get addicted to the drinking itself, because it makes you feel that way.

Addictive personality
possessing certain genes and traits that make you more at risk than other people to become an addict

The thing is, not everybody ends up an adrenaline junkie and does crazy things to get the rush. Some psychologists and doctors think there is a certain kind of personality that makes some people more likely to get addicted. They call it an *addictive personality,* meaning you have certain genes and personality traits that make you more at risk to become an addict than other people.

Jessica An addictive personality? Meaning some kids are *already* at a disadvantage to become addicted?

Ryan There are several traits of the addictive personality. These include being a person who doesn't like to admit weaknesses, always sees other people as responsible for his problems, is an all-or-nothing type, does stuff on a whim without thinking it over, thinks bad things happen to him because they were meant to happen, pays attention only to things that concern him, obsesses about things that don't matter, is passive and doesn't go after what he wants, or lives in the past or future instead of today. Then, if your parents are addicts, experts say you might inherit that "addict gene" too.

Ashley Oh, so kind of like what I've read—that kids who are overweight are more likely to have overweight parents, and kids who become alcoholics often have a parent who was an alcoholic.

Eric On the other hand, lots of other experts are now saying there's no such thing as an "addictive personality." So, the debate is on.

Building Up to It
When Do Kids Start Doing Risky Things?

Ryan My mom says kids are most likely to start doing dumb things when they're most vulnerable—when they feel unsure, when things are changing around them quickly, or when they're uncomfortable with themselves. So, major times of change are really important—like going from elementary school to middle school, to junior high, and of course, to high school. When that happens, chances are you will change, and you might find yourself hanging with completely different people. That means new opportunities, but also facing unknown stuff and even starting from scratch.

Ashley Hey, that actually reminds me of something kinda cool my nana told me. The word *change* in Chinese means both "opportunity" and "danger." Isn't that interesting?

Jessica That's totally neat, Ash.

But I agree. Most eleven- and twelve-year-olds deal with a bunch of changes and have a lot on their minds. Like changing schools, learning the ropes, the whole puberty thing, new interests—and they have no control over most of that stuff. When my sister first started junior high a couple of years back, she was, like, a mess. She was so hard to be around—like constant PMS. We used to fight all the time. And now that she's in high school, she's a nervous wreck.

Eric Yeah, that's totally normal. When people feel vulnerable and not in control, they flip out. I mean, eleven- and twelve-year-olds often say and do things they don't mean or they regret later—because they're totally stressing about everything.

Plus, making mistakes and taking risks—that's all part of growing up. And everybody else around you is older and more experienced, knows what's going on, and has the hang of it much better, so you're kind of at their mercy too. If they're a bad influence or just take advantage of you, you might not catch on until it's too late. So, it makes it that much easier to get pulled into something that's not good.

Ryan When kids are at a vulnerable period, things that make you feel better or more in control are really tempting. High-risk things can help you deal with feeling insecure, out of place, or down in the dumps. You get that adrenaline rush that makes you feel better. And if other kids are cheering you on, it gives you that sense of belonging. Not to mention, it's a great way to distract yourself from whatever's bothering you.

Emile Yeah, tell me about it. I ought to know—I did it all, trying to wipe out my emotional pain and feel more in control. Me and my peeps would roam the streets wreaking havoc—drugs, girls, stolen cars, swiping stuff from mini-marts, graffiti on people's mailboxes. Kept me away from home and my mind off the crap I was constantly getting from my stepfather. And other kids feared us and stepped aside to make way for us. I thought I was hot stuff until I went to jail after a fistfight with my stepdad. And then, all of a sudden, all my peeps disappeared! Nobody had my back anymore.

Ryan Yeah, and you don't have to be eleven or twelve. The teen years are always tough, even if you are one of the "older, more experienced" kids and you seem to have it together. There's just so much pressure, and you gotta manage it all. With my brother, it was too much stress, and he didn't know how to deal. He reached a breaking point and cracked. Couldn't talk to anyone—thought my parents wouldn't understand and would be disappointed. So, he kept it all in and this, like, panic just kept growing. He was looking for some way—any way—to keep it together on the outside, but he was falling apart on the inside. So he found some things to make him let go and forget about it. And they killed him. The whole time, I knew something was wrong. I just didn't know what or what to do about it. After he died, it all came out. His girlfriend spilled it all but too late. It's hard living with that sometimes, knowing maybe I could've done something.

Playing with Fire *Consequences and Repercussions of High-Risk Behaviors and Addiction*

Karen Ry, it wasn't your fault or your responsibility—it was his.

Eric Every risky behavior has consequences. You always pay a price sooner or later. Some bad things that can happen are getting in with the wrong crowd, getting out of control, putting yourself or your future in danger, hurting other people, getting in trouble, and getting hurt or even killed. Living on the edge might sound cool at first. But if you think about all this stuff, it doesn't sound like that much fun. You know what they say: "Live fast, die young!" Remember James Dean? Or is Tupac more your thing? Point is, neither of them has much to say these days.

Emile Yeah, I just got lucky, I think. Glad I put on the brakes when I did. Otherwise, I probably wouldn't be here now. People don't get how serious it can be and how quickly it can get out of hand. Especially if you get addicted. Then, not only are you doing all this stupid stuff, but on top of that, you're not in charge anymore. You're just a puppet, and your addiction is running the show.

Jessica Well, we already talked a lot about the bad consequences of drinking, smoking, doing drugs, eating disorders, and self-injury. I want to talk more about shoplifting, stealing, breaking and entering, fighting, and stuff like that. Some kids just can't resist, even if they have everything and know better.

Karen Most of that stuff is obviously breaking the law big time. If you get caught and go to jail, people will look at you like a criminal and a lot of doors will close in your face. It's, like, totally embarrassing and humiliating. Even if you get a second chance with some things, you won't with others, like the colleges you can go to or the jobs you can get.

Not to mention all the people in your life who'll feel cheated and disappointed—your parents, your friends, all the people close to you. Your reputation goes to hell and everyone is gonna judge you for that one mistake. Some mistakes you just can't undo.

Emile Acting out, getting into fights, joining gangs—they can have many bad consequences too. It doesn't mean you are stronger or better—it just means you use your fists to solve problems instead of your brain. And also that you believe in having power over people by intimidating them instead of having real relationships based on trust and respect. If you get used to hurting other people, you get more and more violent until you end up seriously hurting someone or going to jail. You might also get in over your head, pick a fight you can't win, and get badly hurt yourself.

Taking or destroying other people's property for a rush can also get you a criminal record. The false high makes you go against your instincts and what you know is right. It hardly ever ends well.

If stuff like that doesn't catch up with you now, it can lead you into a life of crime and definitely get you later, when you end up a career criminal. Gambling with your life every day, looking over your shoulder—you can pretty much kiss any chance of having a normal life good-bye.

Startling facts

Every year, 870,000 girls age fifteen to nineteen years old become pregnant. And of the 18.9 million new cases of STDs that happened in 2000, 9.1 million (48 percent or almost half) were among people ages fifteen to twenty-four.

Karen Okay, what about unprotected sex? I know all these girls who think it's so romantic to get "caught up in the moment." Then, nine months later, they're mommies. Guys think it's one more notch on their belt. And then, all of a sudden, they have HIV, and then what? Getting pregnant or getting a *sexually transmitted disease (STD)* is serious business. Every year, 870,000 girls fifteen to nineteen years old become pregnant.[3] If you don't use protection, you're 90 percent more likely to become pregnant within a year. Also, something like 18.9 million new cases of STDs happened in 2000, and 9.1 million (48 percent—almost half) were among people ages fifteen to twenty-four.[4] What's really scary is, in 2004, about 4,883 new people thirteen to twenty-four years old found out they have HIV/AIDS, and about 18,293 kids and teens altogether were living with HIV/AIDS.[5]

Even if you don't get pregnant or an STD, no one ever keeps a secret. And with girls, it gets all over school, and you get a "reputation" for being a slut.

Jessica Yeah. And what's, like, worse is when you put yourself in that kind of situation with someone you don't even know. I have this friend who's addicted to meeting guys and just taking off with them. I keep telling her she's gonna end up in trouble or dead in somebody's trunk. We went to a concert last week, and she meets this guy. Then she, like, ditches me and gets a ride with him. I don't think she even knew his name! Girls get killed doing stuff like that!

Ashley Yeah, I know what you mean. My neighbor got in with this clique, and they go joyriding downtown at night when, like, only the gang bangers and drug dealers are out. I told her once that she's out of her mind—what if their car breaks down, or if they have an accident? They could, like, get kidnapped, raped, beat up, or killed. She said I'm a wuss. I don't care—I like being alive, thank you.

Ryan Gambling—that's another thing. It's like the new craze. My uncle took my cousin to the horse track when he was twelve. Totally stupid! Well, guess what? Now my cousin is $10,000 in debt, and he's only nine-teen. My uncle is whining how he can't find the money to pay off his son's debts. Gambling gives you that ultimate high when you win, so it's very addictive. You end up betting more and more, even when you keep losing. And you're gonna lose more than you win—especially with pro-fessional gambling like poker, blackjack, and roulette. Games of chance are set up that way. You think if you bet once more, you'll hit it big, but before you know it, you're out of luck and out of money. You might end up selling your stuff or stealing from your family just to make your next bet. You lose the trust of people. What's worse, you could get in deep with the wrong people if you borrow money you can't pay back.

Eric Then there are high-risk adventure sports like rock climbing, mountain biking, wild-river rafting, bungee jumping, skydiving, and snowboarding. There are risks that something could go wrong, espe-cially if you aren't prepared, and things can spin out of control quickly. On top of that, lots of kids do the stuff without the protective gear, the required equipment, the right training, or even in the right places, where it's allowed. Some kids will mountain-bike in dangerous areas. Or they'll snowboard without a helmet, or dive off cliffs where there are rocks in the water. Or they'll go down a river they aren't supposed to raft. So, your chances of getting hurt or even killed just went up a gazillion times!

Sure, the sports are technically legal, but what you're doing is causing people to worry about you all the time. Kids end up in the hospital doing stuff like that and some even die.

State-dependent learning

learning things under the influence of a risky behavior that you can't remember or can't do at other times

Ryan Also there's *state-dependent learning* with high-risk behavior. That means you learn how to act under the influence of the risky behav-ior. Because you're "high" and in a different state of mind, when you stop doing the risky behavior, you can't do what you learned or you can't remember what you learned. So, you're not the same person when you're not high.

Not only that. The people you thought were your friends—your "partners in crime"—disappear if you stop doing the risky thing. Turns out they only liked you for what you did, not who you are. You feel really cheated and betrayed—like you were used until your money or whatever else you had going ran out. You end up feeling even worse than before.

Karen Or, when you figure that out, you might decide to continue doing it more and more just to keep the "friends" and the feeling. Before you know it, you're trapped. And that control and independence you were going for? You completely lose that. You aren't in control of anything anymore.

Playing Hide and Seek *Covering Up or Coping with High-Risk Behaviors and Addiction*

Emile Many times, kids know they shouldn't be doing this stuff, and they feel guilty or embarrassed. So, they try to hide their behaviors behind lots of excuses. They pretend like it's no big deal or shut people out when they bring it up. Especially when they're addicted.

In rehab, I learned to take responsibility for my behavior—my drinking, drug use, fighting, stealing, DUI—all if it. Everything I was doing to cope was wrong. Basically, I was using six specific defense mechanisms anyone might use when they don't want to admit they're messing up:

Six Defense Mechanisms for Excusing Bad Behavior

> **Minimizing** Making the results or consequences seem less important or bad than they are
> **Rationalizing** Explaining away and excusing by arguing that when the results are negative or harmful, they were unavoidable anyway
> **Projecting** Transferring our own reasons and motivations for doing something onto others as if they were responsible for our behavior
> **Intellectualizing** Using logic or rational thought to excuse the consequences of the behavior and show why it was a good idea
> **Blaming** Making someone else responsible and guilty for our behavior and the consequences
> **Denying** Simply claiming and insisting it never happened

All of these defenses are "normal"—to protect ourselves. But, when you're doing something you know is wrong and you can't stop, these excuses just help keep the cycle going. Of course, the longer it goes on, the more distance comes between you and the people who don't like what you're doing. Then you work even harder to hide or excuse it. It's a vicious cycle, and you get so caught up in it that you completely lose sight of what matters—your goals and the important people in your life. Don't kid yourself—this is as true with gambling and shoplifting as it is for drugs and booze. Same ball game, just a different court.

Defense Mechanism Examples: *Do You Recognize Yourself or Someone You Know?*	
High-Risk Behavior	**Typical Reactions and the Mechanisms They Involve**
Reckless/drunk driving	***Rationalizing*** "I drive better when I'm high." ***Minimizing*** "It's not a big deal." ***Projecting*** "Everyone does it!" ***Intellectualizing*** "No one I know has ever died after drinking and driving."
Joyriding in a stolen car/ driving recklessly	***Minimizing*** "It's just some harmless fun." ***Rationalizing*** "No one will get hurt." ***Projecting*** "My friends expect me to do it." ***Blaming*** "I have to do this to fit in with my clique."
Shoplifting/stealing	***Projecting*** "A lot of kids do it." ***Denying*** "I don't know what you're talking about." ***Blaming*** "They talked me into it." ***Intellectualizing*** "That lipstick wasn't that expensive." ***Rationalizing*** "That place makes so much money—I can't feel bad for them."
Other delinquent behaviors (vandalizing, breaking and entering, joining gangs, fighting)	***Rationalizing*** "They deserved what they got." ***Denying*** "I didn't do it." ***Blaming*** "I didn't start it—they picked the fight." ***Intellectualizing*** "If you don't stand up for yourself, everybody'll push you around. ***Minimizing*** "It was over before it even started—no one got hurt."
Unprotected sex	***Projecting*** "People do it all the time." ***Rationalizing*** "I didn't have a choice." ***Blaming*** "He made me." ***Intellectualizing*** "I wanted to make him happy." ***Minimizing*** "It was just this one time—it's no big deal."
Exposing yourself to dangerous situations (going to a stranger's house or a bad part of town, running away)	***Minimizing*** "It wasn't really that dangerous." ***Projecting*** "My friend wanted to go—I couldn't just let him go alone." ***Rationalizing*** "I didn't have any other choice." ***Intellectualizing*** "People do it all the time and nothing bad happens." ***Blaming*** "It's my friend's fault—he insisted." ***Denying*** "I can't believe you think I would do something like that!" ***Intellectualizing*** "It was the only way I could make a point." ***Projecting*** "Everything else I do doesn't seem to get through to them."
Gambling	***Rationalizing*** "Hey, it's on the Internet and ESPN, so it's cool!" ***Minimizing*** "It's not like I gamble all the time." ***Intellectualizing*** "Hey, I'm a winner—no worries." ***Projecting*** "My friends play, and they win all the time. ***Blaming*** "If I don't win some money, I'll never be able to afford anything good!"

Ashley Some kids don't even try to deny their behavior or make excuses. They're proud of it—they brag about it and flaunt it like they're heroes or something. Like with drinking or smoking. They show off and try to teach everybody "how it's done."

Jessica Yeah, well, there's something kind of cool about a rebel. A lot of girls *do* go for the dangerous, brooding type of guy. You gotta admit, guys like that *are* kind of hot.

Karen Yeah, the ones you see in movies maybe. But real life isn't like the movies. I doubt it would be all that fun to be arrested with your so-called hot boyfriend for trying to jack a car, or be held up at gunpoint while he gets pounded for not paying his gambling debts.

Uncovering the Truth *The Signs and Symptoms of High-Risk Behavior and Addiction*

Ryan Sometimes, it's real easy to tell when someone is up to no good and messing with things that can hurt them. But other times, they cover it up or blow it off pretty well, so it's not that easy to tell.

Ashley So, how do you know if it's happening—especially if it's your friend or someone you care about? It might even be you who's in too deep, and you just don't know it.

Emile Well, we did group therapy in rehab, and we had to take this quiz. I still have a copy. The questions on it can describe you or someone else. But they're good hints something's not right. People are complicated, so you can have any of these problems at some point and *not* have anything to do with risky behavior or addiction. The trick is when you see four or more of these clues at the same time, you're becoming or are already addicted to something that can really mess you up.

High-Risk Behaviors and Addictions: *Do You Have a Problem?*

> Are you doing something you know—or others have told you—can hurt you or get you in trouble because it gives you a rush, or because you don't want to or can't stop?

> Are you preoccupied with it—do you think about doing it all the time and plan your next "fix" every chance you get?

> Do you find yourself doing it often and even when you're alone—not just when other people are doing it with you or pushing you?

> Do you rush to do it quickly and impulsively, cramming as much of it as you can into a short time, so you can get that instant high?

- Do you keep silent about others who are taking part in it so you can protect your source or support system and make sure you get your next "fix"?
- Do you feel like you are getting more and more used to it, and you need more and more of it to feel the same high?
- Have you lost interest in the people and things that used to matter to you?
- Do you have unpredictable, strong mood swings, outbursts, periods of depression, or feelings you can't control or understand?
- Do you have blackouts (periods of time when you have such mood changes—usually feelings of incredible happiness or sadness—that you don't even remember what happened or remember only the good part of what happened and not all of it)?
- Do you often feel out of control and don't know what to do?
- Do you find yourself sneaking around, lying, telling stories that don't make sense, or shutting out the people who care about you just to hide what you're doing?
- Do you feel embarrassed, ashamed, guilty, or frightened after the high wears off?
- Do you think others definitely will not approve of what you're doing if they knew, and you keep them at a distance?
- Do you feel like your relationships with other people, your well-being, and your future are less important than the thing you're doing?
- Have you gotten hurt or hurt someone else doing what you're doing but still continue?

Emile If you worry that your friend might be in trouble, ask yourself all the questions above, plus these questions:

High-Risk Behaviors and Addictions:
Does Your Friend or Loved One Have a Problem?
- Has your friend or loved one's mood, personality, attitude about life, and/or habits changed a lot really fast, and there's no good explanation?
- Is she acting strange or not like herself in any way that's not explained?
- Is she out of it, absentminded, or "gone with the wind," or is her appearance often unkempt?
- Does your friend sneak around, lie, make up stories that don't add up, or shut people out?
- Has your relationship with your friend suffered or gone bad, and you can't explain why?
- Is your friend making excuses to spend less and less time with you, but spending more and more time with other kids or alone?
- Do you know she's doing something that can hurt her or get her in trouble because it gives her a rush, and she doesn't want to or can't stop?
- Has she asked you to keep her secret and not tell anyone?
- Are you worried that if she doesn't stop, she will end up in jail, seriously injured, or dead?

Emile If you or your friend answered "yes" to four or more of these things, it's very likely you're dependent on or even addicted to something that can cause problems and you or your friend is headed for trouble.

Jessica Okay, so say you take this quiz and you get all these clues that you or someone close to you is up to no good. What then?

First Aid *Helping Yourself* *or a Friend Stop Doing Risky Things*

Eric Well, based on what I've read, there are five things you can do if you have the problem:

Helping Yourself: *Five Things You Can Do Today*

1. *Learn about it.* Find out as much about your problem as you can by researching or talking to other people who have been there. It can help you understand your behavior—whether it's doing drugs, shoplifting, fighting, or running away—and what's causing it. Understanding yourself better can help you deal better with your feelings and your need for the risky behavior.

2. *Create distance.* Cut yourself off from the people who are leading you down that path, encouraging you, or supporting your risky behavior. You don't need that kind of negative reinforcement feeding your addiction.

3. *Don't wait.* If you think you have a problem, reach out for help right away. The longer you wait, the more used to the behavior and dependent on it you get, and it can become a lifeline.

4. *Get it out in the open.* Tell a friend, an older brother or sister, your parents, or another adult you trust, and ask them for help. Anyone you believe cares about you is a good choice, even if you think they might be disappointed or angry. Even if they are, they still love you and will do whatever they can to help you.

   If this makes you nervous, write down your observations and thoughts, and keep track of the behavior on a daily basis. Then you'll know how often you do this behavior, where, to what extent, and what the results are. When you're in the middle of a crisis, everything is confusing and frustrating. Taking time to make notes and reflect will make it easier to sort out your own thoughts and feelings, understand them, and talk to others.

5. *Find other hobbies.* Find fun things to do that give you that same sense of excitement without risking your life and future, or that of others. Playing sports, taking part in competitions, or doing something else that gives you a sense of achievement are good substitutes.

Jessica So, say your friend is doing risky stuff. We all know that, most likely, that person is not going to admit it if she knows it's wrong. And if she is bragging about it and telling everybody, she obviously doesn't think it's bad. So if you talk to her, she'll just excuse it or, like, get pissed at you and avoid you. It would be hard to get her to accept responsibility and stop. What do you do?

Emile There are a bunch of things you can do to help someone who's addicted to risky stuff.

Helping Your Friend: *Seven Things You Can Do Today*

1. **Learn about it.** Find out as much about the problem as you can by researching or talking to other people who have been there. It can help you understand why your friend or loved one might be doing it and what might be behind it. Understanding where your friend is coming from is critical to being able to reach out to him effectively.

2. **Talk to your friend.** Approach your friend in a gentle, caring way and tell him you're concerned about what he's doing. If you want to succeed in helping him see he's in trouble, facts and details about risky situations and what can happen are really helpful. Reminding your friend of the bad things that have already happened to him is also a good way to express your concerns. If you're nervous about talking to him, sending a letter can also be powerful, especially if he's avoiding you.

3. **Really listen.** Most people's favorite thing to talk about is themselves. So, become a good listener and really hear what your friend or loved one is telling you. Listen carefully to what happened, how he feels about it, and what consequences it's causing. You can even take notes so you can remember important things when it's your turn to talk. This also makes the other person feel you're really listening.

4. **Ask questions.** If you aren't sure about something, gently ask questions and make it clear you are there for your friend if he wants to share more details with you. This helps clarify and gives you a better understanding of the situation. It also makes him feel you truly do want to understand where he's coming from. It makes your friend more willing to open up and let you in.

5. **Give your support.** Don't judge, whatever your friend tells you. Let him know you understand and are there for him. Tell him he can always come to you and that you are ready to lend a hand in any way you can. Gently encourage your friend to get help.

6. **Set a positive example.** Let your friend know there are other ways to feel better or get a rush. Some of these include spending quality time with people who love him, playing sports, finding something he likes and excelling at it, or talking through whatever's bothering him instead of keeping it inside and trying to handle it alone.

7. Tell an adult. Tell your parents, your friend's parents, a teacher, a coach, a guidance counselor, a minister, or a family friend you're close to and can count on. It's especially important to tell an adult if your friend is violent or out of control, and you're worried about your own safety if you confront him about the issue. You can ask the adult not to tell your friend it was you who told. An adult, especially someone who works with kids every day, will know what to do and how to help.

Putting on the Brakes before You Go Too Far
Preventing Risky Behavior

Ryan Well, you can't live without any risks, because that's like not living at all. But there's a balance. Sure, some risks are worth it, like taking a chance and telling someone you like them, or entering a competition. But risks that you spend the rest of your life wishing you could undo—or worse, risks you could die from—that's not worth it.

Karen Teenagers think everything's a matter of life and death. But most things aren't. Perspective is everything. If you or someone you care about would suffer or be in serious danger if you don't act, that's the only time it might be okay to risk getting hurt. And that's pretty rare.

The point is to use your brain. Think real hard about the consequences of your decision before you jump into it. Ask yourself if you're doing it for the right reason. Remember, what feels good in the moment doesn't always equal what's good for you. So, don't rush into things before you've had a chance to think long and hard.

Handy tip
Consider the reasons why you should or shouldn't do something—make a list, check it twice.

Eric I found when I'm not sure something's a good idea, especially if I'm being pressured, it's really helpful to make a list. Write down all the pluses and minuses. That way, you can compare them, and it's clearer what the right choice is. Also, you can show the list to friends who might be pressuring you or getting pressured themselves. Everybody likes proof, and it gives you a stronger case for not doing something. Might give them something to think about too.

Ryan Another thing that helps is to follow your gut. Most of the time, when we're about to do something wrong, we get that uneasy feeling something isn't right. Listen to that feeling. If you're getting vibes that it's a bad idea, it probably is. So, don't ignore the little voice. It's like an internal alarm system that helps keep you safe.

Eric Also, if you're really the thrill-seeker type who needs to challenge yourself all the time and you just *have* to do those adventure sports, there's a right way and a wrong way. Make sure to follow the rules, get good training, use all the safety equipment, and don't ignore instructions. That helps keep you safer and can save your life.

Where to Get Help

Jessica So, say I've got this friend who realizes he's in trouble and does want to get help. Where can he, like, turn?

Emile The Internet and the public library have good information, and the phone book lists local crisis centers. Many groups can help for free. Most county and state government offices also have information and helpful services or hotlines you can call to find places that deal with your particular issue. You don't even have to tell them who you are. Just say, "I've got this friend who...has a problem with...whatever. How can I get some help for him?"

Also, some schools have a student assistance program (SAP) that's free for the first several sessions. They know about local resources, so they can send you to someone who specializes in your problem.

Karen There's also this great teen Web site we've talked about a lot before—TeenCentral.Net—created by the children's organization KidsPeace. It's safe, it's screened by experts, and you don't have to give your name.

Emile Speaking of KidsPeace, a friend of mine was kind of out of control, and he went there. They helped him work out his feelings and issues. He's doing much better now. His grades are up, his temper is under control, and his future is looking good.

Ryan There are also several really good crisis hotlines that you or your friend can call and a whole bunch of other hotlines if you think things in your life are getting out of hand. No one has to know your name or where you're calling from.

Web Sites

TeenCentral.Net
www.TeenCentral.Net
This free, anonymous teen Web site by the children's charity KidsPeace gives you a safe place to swap stories with kids from all over the world who are dealing with similar struggles and to find healthy alternatives to high-risk behaviors.

KidsPeace
www.KidsPeace.org
The Web site of the 125-year-old children's charity contains information about a variety of problems and issues you might be facing that could drive you to do risky things.

Teen Help-411
www.child.net/teenhelp.htm
This Web site by the Streetcats Foundation for children in crises provides emergency hotlines and organizations that can help you face and overcome high-risk behaviors that threaten your life, health, or happiness, and the problems that might be causing them.

Kids-in-Crisis
www.geocities.com/heartland/bluffs/5400
This Web ring carries extensive lists of hotlines, links to organization, government Web pages, other resources, and personal stories of struggles and triumphs to help you understand, stop, or prevent bad choices and risky behavior.

Childhelp
www.childhelpusa.org
This Web site of the children's organization gives a whole lot of information on child abuse or other similar issues you might be facing at home that could push you to act out or behave recklessly, as well as information on how you can get help to end the cycle.

TeenHelp.org
www.teenhelp.org
This teen Web site provides a safe, anonymous place where you can get advice and help from trained professionals to deal with the touchy issues or problems you're facing, as well as more information on the burning topics on your mind.

Hotlines

Crisis Helpline
1-800-233-4357 (for any kind of crisis)

Covenant House Hotline
1-800-999-9999 (for any kind of crisis)

National Child-at-Risk Hotline
1-800-792-5200

Red Cross Crisis Prevention
1-800-435-7669

Teen Help-411
1-800-778-9077

National Runaway Switchboard
1-800-621-4000

Additional Resources

Web Sites

Teen Help, the National Children's Coalition and the Streetcats Foundation
www.child.net

City Kids, the National Children's Coalition and the Streetcats Foundation
www.child.net/citykids.htm

The Teen Information Center, Up to You, Inc.
www.choicesforteens.com

HelpingTeens.org
www.helpingteens.org

Books

Adolescent Risk Behaviors: Why Teens Experiment and Strategies to Keep Them Safe (Current Perspectives in Psychology) by David A. Wolfe, Peter G. Jaffe, and Claire V. Crooks

At Risk: Bringing Hope to Hurting Teens by Scott Larson

The Romance of Risk: Why Teenagers Do the Things They Do by Lynn E. Ponton

The Culture of Adolescent Risk-Taking by Cynthia Lightfoot

Getting a Clue: (The Bottom Line Approach for "At Risk" Teens) by Trevor M. Hulse

Shouting at the Sky: Troubled Teens and the Promise of the Wild by Gary Ferguson

Helping Kids Make Wise Choices and Reduce Risky Behavior by Terri Akin, Gerry Dunne, and Dianne Schilling

Teens in Turmoil: A Path to Change for Parents, Adolescents, and Their Families by Carol Maxym and Leslie B. York

At Risk (Sidestreets) by Jacqueline Guest

The Seven Cries of Today's Teens: Hearing Their Hearts; Making the Connection by Timothy Smith

Winning the War Against Youth Gangs: A Guide for Teens, Families, and Communities by Valerie Wiener

Brain, Personality and Addictive Behaviours: The Nature of Conflict by Radha Venga

Addictive Thinking and the Addictive Personality by Craig Nakken and Abraham J. Twerski

Healing the Addictive Personality: Freeing Yourself from Addictive Patterns and Relationships by Lee Jampolsky

CONTRIBUTORS

Alvin F. Poussaint, M.D.
> National Director, KidsPeace Lee Salk Center for Research
> Professor of Psychiatry, Associate Dean, Harvard Medical School
> Director, Media Center, Judge Baker Children's Center

Dr. Poussaint serves as National Director of the KidsPeace Lee Salk Center for Research, which brings together noted authorities in child care to research and develop solutions to social and developmental challenges children and families face today. Dr. Poussaint attended Columbia University and received his medical degree from Cornell University. He took postgraduate training at the UCLA Neuropsychiatric Institute, where he was Chief Resident in Psychiatry. Later, Dr. Poussaint served as the Tufts Medical School director of the psychiatry program and the Director of the Media Center at the Judge Baker Children's Center in Boston. Now at Harvard University, he is a noted expert on children, race relations in America, and issues of diversity, as well as a prolific writer who has published hundreds of articles. Dr. Poussaint is a distinguished life fellow of the American Psychiatric Association, a fellow of the American Association for the Advancement of Science, a member of the American Academy of Child & Adolescent Psychiatry, and a fellow of the American Orthopsychiatric Association. He has received numerous awards and is the recipient of many honorary degrees.

Lewis P. Lipsitt, PH.D.
> National Director, KidsPeace Lee Salk Center for Research
> Professor Emeritus, Brown University
> Founding Director, Brown University Child Study Center

A nationally recognized authority on child development, Dr. Lipsitt is National Director of the KidsPeace Lee Salk Center for Research along with Dr. Poussaint. Honored the world over for his accomplishments and contributions in the field, Dr. Lipsitt is Professor Emeritus of Psychology, Medical Science, and Human Development at Brown University. He is responsible for founding and directing the highly respected Brown University Child Study Center from 1966 to 1991. Dr. Lipsitt is the founding editor of the well-known series *Advances in Child Development and Behavior.* Past Executive Director for Science of the American

Psychological Association, Dr. Lipsitt is the recipient of various distinguished awards, including the prestigious Mentor Award for Lifetime Achievement from the American Association for the Advancement of Science. He also holds a number of citations and honorary degrees for his work and expertise.

C.T. O'Donnell II
KidsPeace President and CEO

C.T. O'Donnell II is President and CEO of KidsPeace. In more than a quarter-century of service as the leader of major national and statewide nonprofits, he has contributed significantly to improving the health, well-being, and education of children. He earned both master's and advanced level sixth-year academic degrees from Duquesne University and undergraduate degrees from Wheeling Jesuit University. Mr. O'Donnell serves on the board of directors of the Child Welfare League of America, on the Families International board, and as a director of the Alliance for Children. He also contributes to the Neuroscience, Listening Post, and Scenario Planning initiatives of human services nonprofits. He has established several organizations focused on helping children and families and is cofounder of the CEO Roundtable for Children, the Renaissance Roundtable for Children, and Child Ways. He has also served as President of the National Organization on Adolescent Pregnancy and Parenting, and as a member of the National Association of Homes and Services for Children.

Lorrie Henderson, PH.D., L.C.S.W.
KidsPeace Chief Operating Officer

Lorrie Henderson has been the Chief Operating Officer at KidsPeace since 2002. For much of his career, Dr. Henderson has devoted his life to helping children. Dr. Henderson is a licensed clinical social worker, has a PH.D. in social work, and has his master of business administration as well as his master's in social work. Prior to his current position, Dr. Henderson was President and CEO of Crittenton Services, Inc. and Vice President of the Florida Sheriffs Youth Ranches, Inc. Dr. Henderson is a published author and editor for *Administration in Social Work, Residential Treatment for Children and Youth,* and *Families in Society.* He is on the board of trustees of the National Association of Psychiatric Health Systems and the National Network of Social Work Managers, and has served on the advisory council of the Joint Commission on Accreditation of Healthcare Organizations.

Joseph A. Vallone, C.F.R.E.

KidsPeace Executive Vice President for Strategic Advancement

Joseph Vallone has served as the key Strategic Advancement Officer for KidsPeace since 1990. During that time, Mr. Vallone cofounded the KidsPeace Lee Salk Center for Research and provided leadership in the creation of National KidsDay®, National Family Day®, and National Family Month®. He also spearheaded the creation of TeenCentral.Net. He graduated from Manhattan College in 1975 with a B.A. in Urban Affairs, later pursuing management and business studies at New York University and planned giving studies at Kennedy Sinclair Institute. Before KidsPeace, he served as Vice President of Development for Muhlenberg Regional Medical Center and Chief Operating Officer for the Diabetes Center of New Jersey. He is a current board member of the Harold B. and Dorothy A. Snyder Foundation and has been honored as a New York Urban Fellowship recipient.

The following additional KidsPeace employed or affiliated child development experts contributed in major ways their professional, clinical, and hands-on knowledge, expertise, and perspectives to developing the content of this work:

Jana Hill, R.D., L.D.N., C.D.E.

Clinical Dietician, KidsPeace

Jana Hill has been a clinical dietician for KidsPeace for ten years, her primary duties involving the provision of nutritional counseling and education to teens, many of whom have eating disorders. She has more than ten years of experience with nutrition and dieting.

Annita B. Jones, PSY.D.

KidsPeace Consultant

Annita B. Jones, PSY.D., worked as a psychologist for the KidsPeace residential program for ten years and provided leadership in the eating disorder, post-traumatic stress disorder (PTSD), and dissociative disorder tracks. She has been in the mental health field for more than thirty-five years.

Peter Langman, PH.D.

Director of Psychology, KidsPeace

Peter Langman, PH.D., has worked with KidsPeace for eight years and has more than twenty years of experience working with children and adolescents. He has authored many works in the field of child welfare, and his expertise has been cited by numerous print, broadcast, and electronic media outlets.

Julius L. Licata, PH.D.
Director, TeenCentral.Net

Julius Licata has been working with children for more than thirty years, initially as a Catholic priest and later as a mental health professional at KidsPeace. He now manages KidsPeace's award-winning teen Web site.

Herbert Mandell, M.D.
National Medical Director, KidsPeace
Medical Director of The KidsPeace Children's Hospital

Herbert Mandell, M.D., provides medical oversight of all KidsPeace programs, which serve some 5,000 children a day at sixty-five centers nationwide. Dr. Mandell has worked with KidsPeace since 1995 and has more than twenty-five years of experience with children.

Janet Sterba, L.P.C.
Clinical Supervisor, Dual Diagnosis Residential Program, KidsPeace

Janet Sterba has worked at KidsPeace for more than twelve years during her twenty-two-year career in child development. She helped design and open the Dual Diagnosis Residential Program for Adolescents in Pennsylvania.

Mary Ann Swiatek, PH.D.
Psychologist, KidsPeace

Mary Ann Swiatek, PH.D., has been a psychologist at the KidsPeace residential treatment program since 2005, having worked for the KidsPeace Children's Hospital since 2001. She specializes in the areas of intellectually gifted children and self-injurious behavior.

David E. Woodward, L.C.S.W., C.A.C.
Executive Director, Hospital & Intensive Residential Programs, KidsPeace

David Woodward has worked with KidsPeace in the area of administration for thirteen years and with children for more than thirty years. He has also worked as an adjunct faculty member at various universities.

Nirmala Yarra Karna, M.D.
Child Psychiatrist, KidsPeace

Nirmala Yarra Karna, M.D., has been working with children for more than twenty years. She has extensive knowledge, training, and expertise in the area of addictions.

Chapter 1: Toasting the Town

1. "Alcohol Use," in *Results from the 2001 National Household Survey on Drug Abuse: Volume 1. Summary of National Findings* (Rockville, MD: Substance Abuse and Mental Health Services Administration, 2002), http://www.oas.samhsa.gov/nhsda/2k1nhsda/vol1/Chapter3.htm (accessed May 2007).

2. Center on Alcohol Marketing and Youth, "Underage Drinking in the United States: A Status Report, 2005," http://camy.org/research/status0306/.

3. "Beer Use," in *PRIDE Questionnaire Report for Grades 6 thru 12: 2002–2003 PRIDE Surveys National Summary/Total* (Bowling Green, KY: PRIDE Surveys, 2003), http://www.pridesurveys.com/Reports/index.html (accessed May 2007).

4. The Century Council, "Underage Drinking Fact Sheet," http://www.centurycouncil.org/underage/65_data.html (accessed May 2007).

5. Ibid.

6. Focus Adolescent Services, "Alcohol and Teen Drinking," http://www.focusas.com/Alcohol.html (accessed May 2007).

7. National Institute on Alcohol Abuse and Alcoholism, "FY 2005 Hearing on Substance Abuse and Mental Health—Director's Statement Before the House Appropriations Subcommittee; Statement by Ting-Kai Li, M.D., Director," http://www.niaaa.nih.gov/AboutNIAAA/CongressionalInformation/Testimony/about_292004.htm (accessed May 2007).

8. The Century Council, "Underage Drinking Fact Sheet."

9. Focus Adolescent Services, "Alcohol and Teen Drinking."

10. L. D. Johnston, P. M. O'Malley, and J. G. Bachman, *National Survey Results on Drug Use from the Monitoring the Future Study 1975–1997. Volume I: Secondary School Students,* NIH Publication No. 98-4345 (Rockville, MD: National Institute on Drug Abuse, 1998); National Clearinghouse for Alcohol and Drug Information, "Youth and Underage Drinking: An Overview," http://ncadi.samhsa.gov/govpubs/RPO990/.

11. Office of National Drug Control Policy and Department of Health and Human Services, "Substance Use in Popular Movies and Music," National Youth Anti-Drug Media Campaign, http://www.mediacampaign.org/publications/movies/movie_partII.html.

12. Jo Anne Grunbaum, Laura Kann, Steven A. Kinchen, Barbara Williams, James G. Ross, Richard Lowry, Lloyd Kolbe, "Youth Risk Behavior Surveillance—United States, 2001," *Morbidity and Mortality Weekly Report* 51, no. SS04 (June 28, 2002): 1–64, http://www.cdc.gov/mmwr/preview/mmwrhtml/ss5104a1.htm.

13. "Types of Alcoholic Beverages Usually Consumed by Students in 9th–12th Grades—Four States, 2005," *Morbidity and Mortality Weekly Report* 56, no. 29 (July 27, 2007): 737–740, http://www.cdc.gov/mmwr/preview/mmwrhtml/mm5629a3.htm.

14. "Substance Abuse," Mental Health America, http://www.nmha.org/index.cfm?objectId=D33166B5-1372-4D20-C84054B1041ED6E8.

15. Associated Press, "Study: College Drinking in 1,400 Deaths," CNN.com, April 9, 2002, http://archives.cnn.com/2002/fyi/teachers.ednews/04/09/us.college.drinking.ap/.

16. Parenting with Dignity, "Drug and Alcohol Abuse," Warning Signs, http://www.warningsigns.info/drugs_warning_signs.htm; American Academy of Child and Adolescent Psychiatry, "Teens: Alcohol and Other Drugs," Facts for Families, http://www.aacap.org/publications/factsfam/teendrug.htm (accessed May 2007).

17. McKinley Health Center at the University of Illinois at Urbana-Champaign, "Approaching Someone about a Suspected Drinking Problem and Communicating Your Concerns," http://www.mckinley.uiuc.edu/handouts/drinking%5fproblem%5fsuspected.html.

Chapter 2: Huffing and Puffing and Blowing the House Down

1. Nemours Foundation, "Smoking Stinks!," KidsHealth for Kids, http://www.kidshealth.org/kid/watch/house/smoking.html (accessed May 2007).

2. Ibid.

3. American Lung Association, "Smoking 101 Fact Sheet," http://www.lungusa.org/site/pp.asp?c=dvLUK9O0E&b=39853.

4. American Cancer Society, "Child and Teen Tobacco Use," Prevention and Early Detection, http://www.cancer.org/docroot/PED/content/PED_10_2X_Child_and_Teen_Tobacco_Use.asp?sitearea=PED (accessed May 2007).

5. Joy Miller, "The Silent Epidemic—Teen Smoking," http://www.centralillinoisproud.com/content/fulltext/?sid=4f989855342afaea8c2eed5ec3c9afe6&cid=1259 (accessed May 2007); American Academy of Family Physicians, "Smokeless Tobacco: Tips on How to Stop," http://familydoctor.org/online/famdocen/home/common/addictions/tobacco/177.html (accessed May 2007).

6. Miller, "The Silent Epidemic—Teen Smoking"; American Academy of Family Physicians, "Smokeless Tobacco"; Ernest Dichter, "Why Do We Smoke Cigarettes?" as quoted at http://smokingsides.com/docs/whysmoke.html (accessed May 2007).

7. Nemours Foundation, "Smoking," TeensHealth, http://www.kidshealth.org/teen/drug_alcohol/tobacco/smoking.html (accessed May 2007); American Lung Association, "Smoking and Teens Fact Sheet," http://www.lungusa.org/site/pp.asp?c=dvLUK9O0E&b=39871 (accessed May 2007).

8. American Cancer Society, "Child and Teen Tobacco Use."

9. Ibid.

10. Research Center, Campaign for Tobacco-Free Kids, http://tobaccofreekids.org/research (accessed May 2007).

11. Nemours Foundation, "Smoking Stinks!"

12. American Cancer Society, "Child and Teen Tobacco Use"; Susan Farrer, "Alternative Cigarettes May Deliver More Nicotine Than Conventional Cigarettes," *NIDA Notes* 18, no. 2 (August 2003).

13. Ibid.

14. Reuters, "Water Pipes, Smokeless Tobacco Harmful, WHO Warns," iVillage Total Health, May 31, 2006, http://heart.health.ivillage.com/newsstories/waterpipessmokelesstobaccoharmfulwho.cfm.

15. American Cancer Society, "Child and Teen Tobacco Use"; Susan Farrer, "Alternative Cigarettes May Deliver More Nicotine Than Conventional Cigarettes."

16. Scott J. Turner, "Study Suggests Smoking May Be a Marker for Potential Drug Abuse, Depression among Adolescents," http://www.brown.edu/Administration/George_Street_Journal/teensmoke.html (accessed May 2007).

17. Ibid.

18. Alan I. Trachtenburg and Michael F. Fleming, "Diagnosis and Treatment of Drug Abuse in Family Practice," National Institute on Drug Abuse, http://www.drugabuse.gov/Diagnosis-Treatment/diagnosis.html.

19. Ibid.

20. Scott J. Turner, "Study Suggests Smoking May Be a Marker for Potential Drug Abuse, Depression among Adolescents."

21. American Cancer Society, "Guide to Quitting Smoking," Prevention and Early Detection, http://www.cancer.org/docroot/PED/content/PED_10_13X_Guide_for_Quitting_Smoking.asp.

Chapter 3: Smoking, Injecting, Snorting . . . Your Life Away

1. Nemours Foundation, "Marijuana," TeensHealth, http://www.kidshealth.org/teen/drug_alcohol/drugs/marijuana.html (accessed May 2007).

2. Wikipedia, "Drug Paraphernalia," http://en.wikipedia.org/wiki/Drug_paraphernalia (accessed May 2007).

3. Substance Abuse and Mental Health Services Administration, *Results from the 2001 National Household Survey on Drug Abuse: Volume I. Summary of National Findings,* NHSDA Series H-17, DHHS Publication No. SMA 02-3758 (Rockville, MD: Office of Applied Studies, 2002).

4. Youth Program Central, Teen Help Adolescent Resources, http://www.vpp.com/teenhelp/index.html (accessed May 2007).

I've Got This Friend Who...

5. Office of National Drug Control Policy, "Marijuana," Drug Facts, http://www. whitehousedrugpolicy.gov/drugfact/marijuana/index.html (accessed May 2007); Publishers Group, "Depressants," http://www.streetdrugs.org/depressants.htm (accessed May 2007).

6. National Institute on Drug Abuse, "Marijuana Abuse," Research Report Series, NIH Publication No. 05-3859 (Rockville, MD: National Clearinghouse on Alcohol and Drug Information, 2005).

7. Office of National Drug Control Policy, "Marijuana"; Substance Abuse and Mental Health Services Administration, *Results from the 2005 National Survey on Drug Use and Health: National Findings*, NSDUH Series H-30, DHHS Publication No. SMA 06-4194 (Rockville, MD: Office of Applied Studies, 2006).

8. University of Michigan, "Monitoring the Future," http://www.monitoringthefuture.org (accessed May 2007). Monitoring the Future, funded by NIDA, is an ongoing study of eighth-, tenth-, and twelfth-grade students. Approximately 50,000 are surveyed each year about their attitudes and actions.

9. National Institute on Drug Abuse, "Opiates," *Mind Over Matter Teacher's Guide,* http://www.nida. nih.gov/MOM/TG/momtg-opiates.html (accessed May 2007).

10. National Institute on Drug Abuse, "Heroin," NIDA InfoFacts, http://www.drugabuse.gov/ InfoFacts/heroin.html (accessed May 2007).

11. Office of National Drug Control Policy, "Heroin," Drug Facts, http://www.whitehousedrugpolicy. gov/drugfact/heroin/index.html.

12. National Institute on Drug Abuse, "Heroin."

13. National Institute on Drug Abuse, "Stimulants," NIDA for Teens, http://teens.drugabuse.gov/ drnida/drnida_stim1.asp (accessed May 2007).

14. Office of National Drug Control Policy, "Cocaine," Drug Facts, http://www. whitehousedrugpolicy.gov/drugfact/cocaine/index.html (accessed May 2007).

15. DEA Demand Reduction, "Methamphetamine," http://www.justthinktwice.com/drugfacts/ methamphetamine.cfm (accessed May 2007).

16. University of Michigan, "Monitoring the Future," http://monitoringthefuture.org (accessed May 2007).

17. National Institute on Drug Abuse, "Ecstasy," Facts on Drugs, NIDA for Teens, http://teens. drugabuse.gov/facts/facts_xtc1.asp; National Institute on Drug Abuse, "MDMA (Ecstasy)," www. nida.nih.gov/DrugPages/MDMA.html.

18. Office of National Drug Control Policy, "Hallucinogens," Drug Facts, www.whitehousedrugpolicy. gov/drugfact/hallucinogens/index.html.

19. DanceSafe, "What Are Magic Mushrooms?" www.dancesafe.org/documents/druginfo/ mushrooms.php (accessed May 2007).

20. U.S. Drug Enforcement Administration, "Inhalants,"www.usdoj.gov/dea/concern/inhalants.html.

21. University of Michigan, "Monitoring the Future."

22. National Institute on Drug Abuse, "Community Drug Alert Bulletin: Prescription Drugs," www. drugabuse.gov/PrescripAlert/CDABprescrip.pdf (accessed May 2005).

23. CA Department of Justice, "Depressants," www.stopdrugs.org/depressants.html (accessed May 2007).

24. Lloyd D. Johnston, Patrick M. O'Malley, Jerald G. Bachman, and John E. Schulenberg, *Monitoring the Future National Results on Adolescent Drug Abuse: Overview of Key Findings, 2005,* NIH Publication No. 06-5882 (Bethesda, MD: National Institute on Drug Abuse, 2006), http:// monitoringthefuture.org/pubs/monographs/overview2005.pdf (accessed May 2007).

25. The National Alliance of Advocates for Buprenorphine Treatment, "Fentanyl," http://naabt. org/documents/fentanyl.pdf; National Institute on Drug Abuse, "Fentanyl," www.drugabuse.gov/ drugpages/fentanyl.html (accessed May 2007).

26. National Institute on Drug Abuse, "Club Drugs," http://www.drugabuse.gov/DrugPages/ Clubdrugs.html (accessed May 2007).

27. National Institute on Drug Abuse, "Epidemiologic Trends in Drug Abuse," Advance Report, June 2000, http://www.drugabuse.gov/CEWG/AdvancedRep/6_20ADV/0600adv.html; Join Together, "Street Drug Prices Hit 20 Year Low," December 6, 2004, http://www.jointogether.org/news/ research/summaries/2004/street-drug-prices-hit-20-low.html (accessed May 2007).

28. National Institute on Drug Abuse, "Hospital Visits," NIDA InfoFacts, http://www.drugabuse. gov/infofacts/HospitalVisits.html (accessed May 2007).

29. Department of Health and Human Services, Centers for Disease Control and Prevention, "Impaired Driving," Injury Center, http://www.cdc.gov/ncipc/factsheets/drving.htm; U.S. Department of Justice, Office for Victims of Crime, "Drunk and Drugged Driving" in *2005 National Crime Victims' Rights Week Resource Guide*, NCJ 207049, http://www.ojp.gov/ovc/ncvrw/2005/pg5g.html (accessed October 2006).

30. U.S Department of Justice, Bureau of Justice Statistics, "Drug Use and Crime," http://www.ojp.usdoj.gov/bjs/dcf/duc.htm.

31. Elizabeth Crane, with assistance from Mindy Herman-Stahl, "Disposition of Emergency Department Visits for Drug-Related Suicide Attempts by Adolescents: 2004," *The New Dawn Report* no. 6 (2006), http://dawninfo.samhsa.gov/files/Suicide_Attempts_%20Adolescents2004_edited.htm.

32. National Institute on Drug Abuse, "Marijuana," NIDA InfoFacts, http://www.drugabuse.gov/infofacts/marijuana.html; Genevieve Pham-Kanter, "Substance Abuse and Dependence," in *Gale Encyclopedia of Medicine* (Gale Group, 2002) as quoted at http://www.healthatoz.com/healthatoz/Atoz/common/standard/transform.jsp?requestURI=/healthatoz/Atoz/ency/substance_abuse_and_dependence.jsp; Clare Hanrahan, "Marijuana," in *Gale Group Encyclopedia of Medicine* (Gale Group, 2002), as quoted at http://www.healthatoz.com/healthatoz/Atoz/common/standard/transform.jsp?requestURI=/healthatoz/Atoz/ency/marijuana.jsp.

33. National Institute on Drug Abuse, "Heroin Abuse and Addiction," Research Report Series, NIH Publication No. 05-4165 (Rockville, MD: National Clearinghouse on Alcohol and Drug Information, revised 2005), http://www.drugabuse.gov/ResearchReports/Heroin/Heroin.html (accessed May 2005).

34. *The American Heritage Dictionary of the English Language*, 4th ed., s.vv. "Convulsions," and "Epilepsy."

35. Substance Abuse and Mental Health Services Administration, *Drug Abuse Warning Network, 2003: Area Profiles of Drug-Related Mortality*, DAWN Series D-27, DHHS Publication No. (SMA) 05-4023 (Rockville, MD: Office of Applied Studies, March 2005), https://dawninfo.samhsa.gov/pubs/mepubs/default.asp.

36. National Institute on Drug Abuse, "Heroin," NIDA InfoFacts, http://www.drugabuse.gov/infofacts/heroin.html; Pham-Kanter, "Substance Abuse and Dependence."

37. National Institute on Drug Abuse, "Crack and Cocaine," NIDA InfoFacts, http://www.drugabuse.gov/infofacts/cocaine.html; Pham-Kanter, "Substance Abuse and Dependence"; Peter Gregutt, "Cocaine," in *Gale Encyclopedia of Medicine* (Gale Group, 2002), as quoted at http://www.healthatoz.com/healthatoz/Atoz/common/standard/transform.jsp?requestURI=/healthatoz/Atoz/ency/cocaine.jsp.

38. National Institute on Drug Abuse, "Methamphetamine," NIDA InfoFacts, http://www.drugabuse.gov/infofacts/methamphetamine.html; Pham-Kanter, "Substance Abuse and Dependence."

39. National Institute on Drug Abuse, "LSD," NIDA InfoFacts, http://www.drugabuse.gov/infofacts/lsd.html; Pham-Kanter, "Substance Abuse and Dependence"; National Institute on Drug Abuse, "Mind Over Matter: Hallucinogens," NIDA for Teens, http://teens.drugabuse.gov/mom/mom_hal1.asp; National Institute on Drug Abuse, "MDMA (Ecstasy)," NIDA InfoFacts, http://drugabuse.gov/infofacts/ecstasy.html; National Institute on Drug Abuse, "PCP (Phencyclidine)," NIDA InfoFacts, http://drugabuse.gov/infofacts/pcp.html.

40. National Institute on Drug Abuse, "Prescription Pain and Other Medications," NIDA InfoFacts, http://www.drugabuse.gov/infofacts/PainMed.html; Pham-Kanter, "Substance Abuse and Dependence."

41. National Institute on Drug Abuse, "Inhalants," NIDA InfoFacts, http://www.drugabuse.gov/infofacts/inhalants.html; Pham-Kanter, "Substance Abuse and Dependence."

42. National Institute on Drug Abuse, "Rohypnol and GHB," NIDA InfoFacts, http://www.drugabuse.gov/infofacts/RohypnolGHB.html; Pham-Kanter, "Substance Abuse and Dependence."

43. McKinley Health Center at the University of Illinois at Urbana-Champaign, "Approaching Someone about a Suspected Drinking Problem and Communicating Your Concerns," http://www.mckinley.uiuc.edu/handouts/drinking%5fproblem%5fsuspected.html.

44. Substance Abuse and Mental Health Services Administration, Office of Applied Studies, "Admissions with Five or More Prior Treatment Episodes: 2002," *The DASIS Report*, October 1, 2004, http://www.oas.samhsa.gov/2k4/manyTx/manyTX.htm.

I've Got This Friend Who...

Chapter 4: A Recipe for Disaster

1. MedicineNet, "Definition of Metabolism," http://www.medterms.com/script/main/art.asp?articlekey=4359 (accessed May 2007).

2. CDC National Center for Health Statistics, "Americans Slightly Taller, Much Heavier than 40 Years Ago," press release, http://www.cdc.gov/od/oc/media/pressrel/r041027.htm (accessed May 2007).

3. Nanci Hellmich, "Do Thin Models Warp Girls' Body Image?" *USA Today,* http://www.usatoday.com/news/health/2006-09-25-thin-models_x.htm (accessed May 2007).

4. Susan Ice and the *Journal of the American Academy of Child and Adolescent Psychiatry,* "Statistics from The Renfrew Center," Eating Disorders Coalition, http://www.eatingdisorderscoalition.org/reports/statistics.html (accessed May 2007); Susan Ice, "Children with Eating Disorders: A Growing Public Health Concern," in *A Congressional Briefing, Not Just a Passing Phase: The Truth about Children and Eating Disorders,* July 24, 2001, http://www.eatingdisorderscoalition.org/congbriefings/072401/housebriefing072401.html#ice.

5. Ibid.

6. Kate Fox, "Mirror, Mirror: A Summary of Research Findings on Body Image," Social Issues Research Centre, http://www.sirc.org/publik/mirror.html (accessed May 2007).

7. MedicineNet, "Definition of Calorie," http://medterms.com/script/main/art.asp?articlekey=8567 (accessed May 2007); Nemours Foundation, "Learning About Calories," KidsHealth for Kids, http://kidshealth.org/kid/nutrition/food/calorie.html (accessed May 2007).

8. American Academy of Family Physicians, "Anorexia Nervosa," http://familydoctor.org/online/famdocen/home/common/mentalhealth/eating/063.html (accessed May 2007); Wikipedia, "Anorexia Nervosa," http://en.wikipedia.org/wiki/Anorexia_nervosa (accessed May 2007).

9. MedicineNet, "Bulimia," http://www.medicinenet.com/bulimia/article.htm (accessed May 2007); U.S. Department of Health and Human Services, "Bulimia Nervosa," WomensHealth.Gov, http://womanshealth.gov/faq/easyread/bulnervosa-etr.htm#a (accessed May 2007).

10. Nemours Foundation, "Binge Eating Disorder," TeensHealth, http://kidshealth.org/teen/food_fitness/problems/binge_eating.html (accessed May 2007); Mayo Foundation for Medical Education and Research, "Binge-Eating Disorder," http://www.mayoclinic.com/health/binge-eating-disorder/DS00608 (accessed May 2007).

11. Susan Ice and the *Journal of the American Academy of Child and Adolescent Psychiatry,* "Statistics from The Renfrew Center."

12. Nemours Foundation, "Eating Disorders," KidsHealth for Parents, http://kidshealth.org/parent/emotions/feelings/eating_disorders.html (accessed May 2007); U.S. National Library of Medicine, "Eating Disorders," Medline Plus, http://www.nlm.nih.gov/medlineplus/eatingdisorders.html (accessed May 2007).

13. MedicineNet, "Definition of Acid Reflux," http://www.medterms.com/script/main.art.asp?articlekey=10173 (accessed May 2007); MedicineNet, "Definition of Esophagus," http://www.medterms.com/script/main.art.asp?articlekey=3326 (accessed May 2007).

14. American Obesity Association, "Childhood Obesity," http://www.obesity.org/subs/childhood/prevalence.shtml (accessed May 2007).

15. Medical News Today, "CDC Downscales Mortality Risk from Obesity, USA," http://www.medicalnewstoday.com/medicalnews.php?newsid=23210 (accessed May 2007).

16. Anorexia Nervosa and Related Eating Disorders, "Statistics: How Many People Have Eating Disorders?" http://www.anred.com/stats.html (accessed May 2007).

17. MedicineNet, "Definition of Fat," http://www.medterms.com/script/main.art.asp?articlekey=3394 (accessed May 2007).

18. United States Department of Agriculture, "MyPyramid Poster for Kids," MyPyramid.gov, http://teamnutrition.usda.gov/Resources/mpk_poster2.pdf.

19. United States Department of Agriculture, "Inside the Pyramid," MyPyramid.gov, http://mypyramid.gov/pyramid/discretionary_calories_amount_table.html.

Chapter 5: Cutting Yourself Down

1. Mayo Clinic Staff, "Self-Injury/Cutting," Mental Health Center, MayoClinic.com, http://www.mayoclinic.com/health/self-injury/DS00775; American Academy of Child and

Adolescent Psychiatry, "Self-Injury in Adolescents," Facts for Families, http://aacap.org/page.ww?name=Self-Injury+in+Adolescents&section=Facts+for+Families.

2. Cornell University Family Life Development Center, "What Do We Know About Self-Injury?" Cornell Research Program on Self-Injurious Behavior in Adolescents and Young Adults, http://www.crpsib.com/whatissi.asp (accessed May 2007).

3. Cool Nurse, "Self-Injury," http://www.coolnurse.com/self-injury.htm (accessed May 2007).

4. Cornell University Family Life Development Center, "What Do We Know About Self-Injury?"

5. Chart adapted from Barrent W. Walsh, *Treating Self-Injury: A Practical Guide* (New York: Guilford, 2006).

6. American Academy of Child and Adolescent Psychiatry, "Self-Injury in Adolescents."

Chapter 6: High-Risk Behavior

1. Centers for Disease Control and Prevention, "Youth Risk Behavior Surveillance—United States, 2005," *Morbidity and Mortality Weekly Report* 55, no. SS-5 (June 9, 2006), http://www.cdc.gov/MMWR/PDF/SS/SS5505.pdf (accessed May 2007).

2. Ibid.

3. Jo Anne Grunbaum, Laura Kann, Steven A. Kinchen, Barbara Williams, James G. Ross, Richard Lowry, Lloyd Kolbe, "Youth Risk Behavior Surveillance—United States, 2001," *Morbidity and Mortality Weekly Report* 51, no. SS04 (June 28, 2002): 1–64, http://www.cdc.gov/mmwr/preview/mmwrhtml/ss5104a1.htm.

4. "STD-Prevention Counseling Practices and Human Papillomavirus Opinions Among Clinicians with Adolescent Patients—United States, 2004," *Morbidity and Mortality Weekly Report* 55, no. 41 (October 20, 2006): 1117–1120, http://www.cdc.gov/mmwr/preview/mmwrhtml/mm5541a1.htm.

5. U.S. Department of Health and Human Services, Health Resources and Services Administration, Maternal and Child Health Bureau, "Adolescent and Young Adult HIV/AIDS," Child Health USA 2006, http://www.mchb.hrsa.gov/chusa_06/healthstat/adolescents/0320ayah.htm.

I've Got This Friend Who...

I've Got This Friend Who...